BE RIGHT BACK!

PUPPY SEPARATION ANXIETY

EDITION

BE RIGHT BACK!

PUPPY SEPARATION ANXIETY EDITION

Your Simple Step-by-Step Guide To Raising an Easy-Going, Independent, Happy-Home-Alone Puppy

Julie Naismith

pitmore
PUBLISHING

ISBN 978-1-9992966-2-9

In order to maintain privacy, the author and publisher have in some instances changed the name and identifying details of individuals. Although the author and publisher have made every effort to make sure all information is correct at press time, the author and publisher do not assume and hereby disclaim any liability to any party for any loss, damage, disruptions caused by stories within this book, whether such information is a result of errors or omission, accident, slander, or other cause.

Information in this book is NOT intended for use as diagnosis or treatment of dog behavior or medical problems, or as a substitute for consulting a licensed veterinarian or a certified dog training professional. Always seek the advice of your veterinarian or other qualified professional for medical or behavioral conditions. Never disregard professional advice or delay in seeking it because of something you read in this book.

Cover image: Nick Ridley Photography
Cover design: Simon Avery
Layout + design: Amanda Baye
Beta readers: Stacey Bell, Vanessa McDonald, and Jessica Ring
Edited by: Jodi Brandon
Indexed by: Balša Delibaši

A NOTE ABOUT TERMINOLOGY

Pronouns

Throughout the book I've applied the masculine him, he, or his when referring to both male and female dogs. This in no way reflects a gender bias, but rather is used for simplicity. Some authors avoid this by referring to a dog as it, but this is not how I, nor most owners, think of dogs.

Describing Our Relationship

In the book, I refer to the dog's human as *owner*. I don't love this term because I don't believe it describes the true relationship we have with our dogs. However, I struggle to find another term that does work.

I find *guardian* comes across as too legal and cold, and in many countries in the world it just doesn't resonate.

Pet parent or *dog mom* do get at the emotional and caring nature of the relationship that certainly I have with my dogs. But I didn't give birth to my dogs so perhaps step-mom is more fitting.

I've also seen the terms *carer* and *caregiver* used but I find these sound too clinical and detached.

In reality I am many things to my dogs: their playmate, their friend, their companion, their provider, their guardian, their caregiver, and their protector. I'm also honored to be their chef, butler, driver, ball thrower, and poop picker-upper. Above all, though, I'm the person who loves them more than anything else in the whole wide world. Until I find a word that can encompass all of that I stick with the conventional term of *owner*.

RESULTS DISCLAIMER

While every effort has been made to accurately represent how to get your puppy over separation anxiety, there is no guarantee that you will. Even though separation anxiety training has a high success rate, there is never any guarantee with behavior change. Any professional who tells you otherwise is not being transparent.

Examples of successful cases in this book are not to be interpreted as a promise of results. Successful resolution is entirely dependent on the person doing the training, and on each individual dog's condition.

To you and your puppy

Puppyhood should be the happiest time in both your lives.

I wrote this book for you in the hope that it helps you enjoy every moment of this precious time.

Let's make this dedication official—write your name and your puppy's name below (even if it's your puppy-to-be!).

TO _____

AND _____

ACKNOWLEDGMENTS

Thanks go again to my family, who continue to encourage and support me every day.

I must thank my wonderful dogs too. They are the best muses and the most charming writing companions, even if their snoring can be a little distracting (and are my books that boring?!)

I'd also like to thank the many professionals who I've been privileged to work with in my SA Pro Trainer certification. The way they make the world a better place for dogs and puppies every single day makes my heart full.

It would have been impossible to write this book without the input of Vanessa McDonald, Jessica Ring, and Stacey Bell who provided a sounding board for my ideas.

In addition, I'm truly grateful for the endless patience of both my brilliant editor, Jodi Brandon, and my fabulous designer, Amanda Baye.

But special thanks go to you for taking the time to learn how to help your puppy be happy home alone. Not only do I thank you for this, but your puppy wanted me to let you know that he says thank you too.

CONTENTS

AUTHOR'S NOTE
Lockdown and Separation Anxiety

At the time of writing, most of us are still dealing with the aftermath of COVID-19 restrictions, whether that was full lockdown or limitations on regular activities.

Lockdown has been hard on our dogs. While they've undoubtedly loved having us around, many dogs have struggled with the cycle of being with us 24/7, seeing us going back to something close to normal, only to go back into lockdown, and so on.

Having their human around for so many months caused many dogs to forget how to be alone. The contrast between having their human around 100% of the time and then them suddenly being gone has been too much for many dogs and puppies to cope with. If your puppy is a pandemic puppy, he might never have known any difference. No wonder then he got upset when you returned to the office.

On top of that, dog walkers have gone out of business, daycares have reduced their hours to cope with less demand, and vets stopped allowing owners to accompany their pets. Family members outside of the household have been restricted from visiting, and for many dogs their worlds got smaller.

They did, however, get more walks, more snuggles, and more human time, so overall the picture has been mixed.

If you're still not back to your normal routine when you read this, or you think that maybe we're not out of the woods yet, then don't worry. You can use the training in this book to both prevent and treat your puppy's separation anxiety. Even if you and your family are home all the time, you can still do the training. The key is to teach your puppy that you do actually leave, that they aren't going to be with you 24/7, and that, when you go, it's always safe and you always come back.

That's what separation anxiety training is all about.

PREFACE

I have one puppy left. The family who reserved her changed their mind last-minute. If you want her, you'll have to collect her tomorrow."

It wasn't meant to be like this. I'm a planner. I'd been planning for a puppy for months. I decided which breed, researched breeders, and met lots of litters. I picked out my perfect puppy when she was four weeks old.

I used the four weeks between me finding her and her coming home to plan even more. I booked time off work, hired a trainer to help me prepare, and arranged for daycares and sitters for when I went back to work.

The excitement killed me!

Then three days before P-Day (Puppy Comes Home Day), the breeder called to say my puppy was sick. She would be okay but wouldn't be able to come home for several weeks, at least.

"Oh" was all I said, as I saw all my plans flying out of the window.

I couldn't wait. Not because I was being impatient (okay, maybe a bit) but because, well, my plans! I couldn't rearrange everything and expect it all to line up again. I needed to give my puppy the best start, and it wouldn't be fair to bring her home to chaos.

The breeder said she'd understand if I wanted to pass. That's what I did.

So, the search began anew.

Then one day before P-Day, I read an email from a breeder I'd visited a few months back. She had a new litter! I called her that minute.

She had a puppy—a puppy who was due to go home on my P-Day, but who was no longer wanted by the original family.

Next thing I knew, I was dashing to the station and heading out of London on a busy commuter train to Essex to visit the breeder.

And that's how I first got to meet India, aka India my perfect puppy.

I'm not sure I believe in fate, but if I did, this would be proof that fate exists. The perfect puppy for me had been turned down by another family, and she was just waiting for me to swoop her home.

Yes, I'm biased. And yes, everyone thinks their puppy is perfect.

While India might not have been perfect, she was the easiest puppy anyone could ever ask for. And I don't say that about all my dogs. Percy couldn't be left. And Tex . . . well, we didn't know him as a puppy. But, as much as we adore him, he is most certainly a difficult adult dog.

India was utterly delightful, sweet, and well-mannered in every single way. She was also chill—so chill, in fact, that when she was about four months old I was concerned that she must be sick. My experience with puppies prior to India was that they were bouncy, crazy balls of energy, so one day I concluded that all the sleeping she was doing was abnormal. I took her to the vet extremely concerned that there was something seriously wrong with my precious pup.

£45 and two hours later, I returned home with the reassurance from the vet that my puppy was nothing more than a chill, sleepy pup.

I was a good puppy mom to India and did all the things: classes, socialization, enrichment, crate training, and teaching her manners.

However, India was one of those puppies for whom I could've done none of those things and she would still have been perfect.

Sometimes as owners we get lucky and have a puppy like India who flatters our dog ownership skills. We don't do everything we should, but they still turn out okay.

But India tricked me. She tricked me into thinking that dog guardianship was easy—so much so that I decided I would like a challenge next time, especially as I'd become interested in dog training and was thinking I would like to be a trainer. I wanted a puppy who was bouncier, squirmier, and more energetic than India. And my goodness did I find that puppy.

Enter Percy (or, as he's often known, "Oh Percy!").

Percy is India's half-brother. But as everyone who knows them points out, they could not be more different in temperament. India will come back every single time she's called, while Percy will evade capture until every single squirrel in every single tree has been thoroughly barked at.

India will doze all day in one of her many "princess beds" until something exciting is happening. Percy will rest for a bit, but then bug you for some fun—cute, and I wouldn't have it any other way, but sometimes the India approach is less taxing.

And when it comes to home-alone time, they could not have been programmed more differently. With India it was just never an issue. I didn't leave her for particularly long periods when she was a puppy, and she spent a lot of time at puppy daycare when I was back at work. When she was left, she was good as gold.

Percy . . . well, home-alone time and Percy did not mix.

For whatever reason, Percy hated being left. He barked,

howled, cried, drooled, salivated, and panted, and he did not calm down until I returned.

Back then I'm not even sure I'd heard the term *separation anxiety*, let alone think that my dog would struggle to be alone. In hindsight, though, I'm pretty sure my childhood dog, Timmy, suffered from home-alone stress. My trickster puppy, India, duped me into believing that dogs are fine on their own.

I did all the same things with Percy that I did with India: all the same training. The same amount of exercise. Attention to crate training. None of that made a bit of difference.

Sadly for Percy and for me, I didn't realize at first that not leaving him was essential if I was ever going to get him over separation anxiety.

Naïve as I was, I did what you might have tried or what you've probably been told to try: I left him to cry it out.

While India took herself off to her crate for chill time when I left, Percy howled.

The headline version of my story with Percy is this: I did get him over separation anxiety, and these days I help people like you get dogs over separation anxiety.

However, chill Miss India is as important a character in this story as Percy. You see, what India made me realize was that, despite what everyone was telling me, it wasn't my ownership style causing Percy's anxiety.

Here are all the things I did with India that people told me could be causing Percy's anxiety:

- I allowed her to sleep on the bed.

- I cuddled her when she wanted to cuddle.

- I gave her attention when she asked for it.

- I didn't buy into the dogs needing to be alpha myth.

- I allowed her on the furniture.

- I let her eat ahead of me.

- I didn't stop her when she tried to
exit the door before I did.

I did all of these things, and yet, whenever I left the house, India was fine.

All of this led me to conclude that:

- Percy wasn't just going to "get over" this,

- I wasn't the cause, and

- I had to take a very different approach
with Percy in order to help him to be
comfortable being home alone.

If it hadn't been for India being my benchmark, I most likely would have concluded that the situation with Percy was my fault—and that it was probably hopeless.

So thank you, India, for showing me that dogs can be alone. Thank you, Percy, for showing me that dogs can go from hating being alone to being perfectly fine.

Without the two of you, I wouldn't be here today helping dogs and their owners overcome separation anxiety.

INTRODUCTION

f you're anything like I was, you didn't plan on having a dog you couldn't leave (though maybe because you're reading this book you're more on top of it than I was!).

Like me, you researched what to do when you bring a puppy home and have read that the three main things you need to focus on are:

1. Housetraining.

2. Socialization.

3. Obedience or manners training.

While these are important, there's one huge piece of learning that's missing from the list: teaching a puppy how to be happy home alone.

We don't ever assume that puppies know not to pee on the carpet. We know that we have to teach them to pee outside and not in the house. Yet we assume (because no one tells us otherwise) that our puppies will be fine on their own and that they don't need any skills to deal with being left at home while their humans are out.

But think about it: Before they come into our homes, they spend the first eight weeks of their life surrounded by other puppies and having lots of contact with humans.

Then we transport them into a completely strange environment and, with almost no prep expect them to settle when we leave them entirely alone.

Coping with being alone is a life skill that puppies must learn, yet no one tells us we need to teach them how to be alone. With most puppies we get lucky, and they grow up into dogs who are fine on their own. Maybe that's why home-alone training isn't a priority.

However, I've seen so many dogs who weren't given home-alone coping skills so, for me, home-alone training is every bit as important as housetraining and socialization. And I'd say it's more important than obedience behaviors.

Your puppy has a lifetime to learn how to sit. But if he doesn't learn how to be home alone, it might take a lifetime to show him how to handle being left.

That's why I believe home-alone training is a must for every puppy checklist.

Since being home alone isn't a natural state, we owe it to our puppies, and dogs, to equip them to handle time without their humans.

That's why this book covers:

- Planning for getting a puppy,

- Preventing home-alone issues in your new puppy, and

- Remedial training for puppies who have been in their new home some time and are struggling with their humans leaving.

The book also covers advice for behaviors that tend to occur alongside or come along for the ride with separation-related issues.

The separation anxiety training method core to this book is

gradual exposure training, and it's based on how we help humans overcome fears.

The specific method I'm going to show you in this book, my SubThreshold Training process, has been used successfully on hundreds of dogs and puppies, so you know that you are getting a tried and trusted method that works.

"

Such short lives our pets have to spend with us, and they spend most of it waiting for us to come home each day.

JOHN GROGAN

CHAPTER 1

All about Puppy Separation Anxiety

We've spent the best part of 30,000 years selecting dogs because of their friendliness and desire to be with us. We love dogs because they love to be with us and are never happier than when in our company (except perhaps when they are in our company *while* chasing squirrels).

We get a puppy because we're looking for companionship. If we wanted a pet who wasn't going to be bonded to us, we'd get a robot dog.

With all that love and bonding, it's no wonder that dogs are disappointed when we leave. I'm not sure a dog exists who *loves* it when we leave.

Unlike humans, who relish a rare night with the place to ourselves, dogs don't dance up and down when we go out.

Rather, they are resigned to our absence, disappointed that we've left, and they go into waiting mode. Puppies get especially disappointed because, like little humans, puppies don't come hardwired with patience and waiting skills.

But being disappointed at being left and being anxious at being left are two very different states.

Separation anxiety is when a dog has a fear of being alone. For some dogs, the fear is so severe that they go into a panic.

The only relief from their fear is your return.

Some dogs are fine as long as someone—any human—is with them. However, based on the polls I've conducted in my free community and on information collected from my several hundred paying clients, about 20% of dogs who suffer from separation anxiety have a need to be with a particular person. They aren't fine with just anyone. It has to be their special person or persons. You might hear this referred to as *hyper-attachment*.

These are the dogs who are glued to your side, no matter where you are in the house. That *doesn't* mean separation anxiety is caused by having an extra-strong bond with your dog. Lots of dogs like to be their owner's shadow but don't panic when their owner leaves the house. Owners who have had multiple normal dogs who were attached to them will tell you they didn't do anything differently with the dog who developed separation anxiety.

For the purposes of this book, *separation anxiety* will refer to both puppies who can't be alone and those who are overly attached to their humans. (The section "Tips for Hyper-Attached Puppies" in Chapter 4 looks at specific tactics for dealing with hyper-attachment.)

In this chapter we look at why fear is a natural state for dogs and how that relates to the likelihood of your puppy having separation anxiety. We consider what you need to look for if you're trying to decide whether your puppy is truly frightened of being left. This chapter also digs into what else might be going on if it's not fear by comparing normal puppy behaviors with anxious ones.

We bust some puppy separation anxiety myths by presenting the facts, and we cover what to look for when you're trying to find reliable advice about your puppy. Finally, we talk about whether you might be contributing to your puppy's anxiety.

Can Puppies Really Get Separation Anxiety?

You're no doubt reading this book because you're worried about your puppy getting separation anxiety.

Or, you're already pretty sure that your puppy does have separation anxiety.

Maybe people have been telling you that you're being ridiculous—that there's no way that your puppy can have separation anxiety. You'll hear people say that your puppy is just going through "normal puppy behavior." The argument is that puppies get upset when left and that your puppy is no different.

However, this simply isn't true.

Let's have a look at why.

Puppies shouldn't be fearful. Between the ages of three and 12 weeks, puppies should be fearless, curious, and ready to explore the world with confidence. This is the same for all young mammals. There is a period in their early development when fear is not a natural state for them. This fearless period allows them to get new experiences. And this exposure to novel experiences sets them up to deal with those experiences later in life. If they were fearful, they wouldn't expose themselves to anything new.

However, fear is actually a natural state for most animals. Here's why.

Imagine a gazelle grazing on the savanna. In the distance she spots another animal and it's not a gazelle.

Before it gets closer, she must decide if it's friend or foe. If it is a predator she must run.

Here are her options (and their potential outcome):

1. Assume it's a predator when it's not.
    The gazelle runs away from something that wasn't going to snack on her.

2. Assume it's a predator when it is.
    The gazelle runs away and escapes becoming lunch.

3. Assume it's not a predator and assume correctly.
    The gazelle safely continues grazing.

4. Assume it's not a predator when it actually is.
    The gazelle is lunch.

In scenarios 1, 2, and 3 the gazelle survives and goes on to breed and pass on genes. Scenario 4 results in a dead gazelle.

Subsequent gazelles learn that assuming something is going to get them, even when it does not, pays off. Being over-confident doesn't pay off.

Hence fear gets passed on, because being fearful keeps you alive.

Dogs are no different. Even though dogs are domesticated and no longer free to breed, fear gets passed down. That is why it is entirely possible for puppies, who should come into the world fearless, to be hardwired for fear-based problems.

Plus, we know neuroscience shows that early life experiences can create fear.

These early life experiences include:

- What happened to the puppy's mum when she was carrying,

- How the puppy's mum related to her puppies,

- Early bad experiences that might have happened to the litter, such as going hungry, being unwell, or being exposed to anything at intensity that scared the puppy, and

- Lack of socialization.

So yes, your puppy could have a true fear of being left. And while many puppies do fuss when left, some do so because they are frightened.

Be a Separation Anxiety Detective

If you're trying to work out what's going on with your puppy, what do you need to be alert to?

The signs we look for when deciding if a puppy has separation anxiety are:

- *Excessive* barking, whining, crying, and howling.

- Chewing or destroying floors, walls, and doors, particularly around entrances.

- Frantic attempts to escape, sometimes to the point of self-harm.

- Soiling (especially when the puppy is otherwise house-trained).

- Getting anxious well before you leave.

It's common to think that a puppy needs to display all these behaviors to be diagnosed with separation anxiety. I often hear owners say, "I don't think it can be separation anxiety because all he does is bark" or "It doesn't seem like separation anxiety because he destroys but the neighbors haven't complained about howling."

In fact, some anxious puppies don't display any of the more common problem behaviors but instead show some of the other signs of fear shown here:

Licking	Panting
Salivating, drooling	Whining, low-level crying
Freezing	Hiding
Withdrawing	Trembling
Eyes wide	Ears pinned back
Tail tucked	Pacing
Cowering	Shaking
Pupils dilated	Excessive grooming
Excessive lip licking	Excessive yawning

What's Normal Puppy Behavior and What's Separation Anxiety?

As you read the bulleted list in the previous section, you no doubt were thinking, "But aren't some of these normal puppy behaviors?" They are, especially chewing and soiling. Puppies love to sink those little needle teeth into anything that feels good, and even the best house-trained puppy might still have the occasional accident when you're not around to swoop them outside when they sniff and circle.

This can be confusing, but the behaviors listed in the previous chart are often more intense and last longer in anxious puppies.

Take the FOMO (fear of missing out) puppy, who can't bear to think there's something exciting going on without him. As soon as you leave, the dog starts to bark. It might begin with a "Hey, I think you might have forgotten me?" but it quickly escalates to a "You can't go out without me!" tantrum. FOMO puppy keeps going until they realize the barking isn't working. They give up and snooze through the rest of your absence.

Then there is the watchdog puppy, whose life's mission is to alert you to threats to your survival, such as the UPS guy. This puppy might try to get to the window to bay at every passerby the entire time you're out. They'll be even more into this type of behavior if you don't let them do it when you're home.

Other home-alone puppies chew because they're bored. Some might soil while you're out, because they've learned that it's safer to pee on the carpet when you're not there to yell at them—or they are just not 100% reliable yet.

None of these puppies are anxious. They may be bored, frustrated, and/or amped up, but they're not in a panic. In other words, they're just getting up to normal puppy stuff.

Contrast those examples with a puppy who has separation anxiety, who is so worried that the barking continues to escalate for the entire time you are gone, or the panicked puppy, who is so upset he rips his nails, trying to dig his way out.

That isn't typical puppy behavior. Puppies are babies and are demanding. But most don't panic when alone, especially after the

❙❙ When the barking comes from fear, the behavior will persist for as long as the fear persists.

first few days (see "Bringing it All Together: Your Puppy's First Week Separation Anxiety Proofing Plan" in Chapter 3).

I categorize this home-alone behavior into *thinking* and *emotional.*

Thinking behavior is the puppy strategizing. If the puppy could talk, we might hear him say, "If I bark loud enough, they might come back and take me for that walk they seem to have forgotten about" or "This table leg looks fun. Think I might settle down and chew on that for the afternoon."

Dogs, like any evolved animals, will put as much effort into a behavior as justifies the outcome. If barking and barking to go out for a walk doesn't eventually result in a walk, the thinking dog will give up. Dogs do what works.

Emotional behavior, on the other hand, has no such calculated logic or intent. Most likely the dog has no control over the behavior. He doesn't think. And it looks like the dog is incapable of stopping.

When the barking or chewing comes from fear, the behavior will persist for as long as the fear persists.

It's a bit like screaming on a roller coaster: It stops when the roller coaster stops.

Patricia McConnell, in her influential book *I'll Be Home Soon,* suggests that the acting-out behaviors may be self-soothing. And therein lies the reward for the effort.

This confusing overlap in home-alone behaviors can confound, but if I had to pick out one key difference between fearful dogs and bored dogs, it is perseverance.

Ask the owner of a dog who has separation anxiety how long their dog does his thing, and the answer is usually "For as long as we're out."

As I explain in this book, each case of separation anxiety is different, and it's hard to generalize. Some dogs display problem behavior intermittently during an absence. The majority do it for the entire time.

BEHAVIOR

Barking	
TYPICAL PUPPY	Might bark when you go but settles easily. Doesn't do it every time you leave.
FRIGHTENED PUPPY	Barks every time you leave. Doesn't give up.

Chewing and destroying	
TYPICAL PUPPY	Chews when you're gone, but it looks more like mischief, like they're looking for fun stuff to get stuck into. You might see a few personal items nibbled or a scatter cushion dissected.
FRIGHTENED PUPPY	Chews when you're gone, but it looks more like destruction or escape. It's frantic and persistent behavior.

Soiling	
TYPICAL PUPPY	Still pretty *unreliable* and have accidents all the time, so little wonder they soil when you're out. It might even seem like they're being sneaky because they do it when your back is turned. More likely, if you've ever scolded them for soiling in the past, they've decided they won't get shouted at if they pee when you're not around.
FRIGHTENED PUPPY	Pretty *reliable* but are suddenly soiling only when you leave, which doesn't add up to you.

CONTEXT

Owner absent / present	
TYPICAL PUPPY	Happens whether you are around or not.
FRIGHTENED PUPPY	Happens only when you're out *or* is worse or more intense when you're out.

Conditions	
TYPICAL PUPPY	Less likely to do when the **SAFE** conditions are met (i.e., when their needs have been met): **S**leepy, **A**ll-played out, **F**ull tummy, **E**mpty bladder.
FRIGHTENED PUPPY	The problem behavior arises when you leave even when all their needs have been met.
	Just like us, panicking puppies don't panic any less just because they're tired or have had a big meal. If you'd completed a long run and eaten a huge meal, the smoke alarm going off at 2 a.m. would still panic you.

Still undecided whether it's separation anxiety or not? No need to worry. The training I cover in the book helps prevent and treat all home-alone issues. My method will increase your puppy's tolerance of being alone, whether the cause is fear or frustration, thinking or emotional behavior.

Fear vs. Anxiety

When a dog has separation anxiety, is it really fear?

Let's look at the difference between anxiety and fear. These definitions are from the American Psychological Association:

- Fear is the experience of a threat.

- Anxiety is the anticipation of a threat.

If you're wandering alone through the woods late at night, you might feel anxious that something bad could happen. If someone jumps out at you while you're wandering in the woods, you would experience fear.

So are dogs worrying about something that might happen to them when you leave (or happen to you, for that matter)? Or are they in the moment fearful about something that could happen to them any minute?

We don't actually know, because we can't ask our dogs whether it's fear or anxiety. And fear and anxiety look very similar.

It concerns me that, as a society, we are more dismissive of anxiety than we are of fear. And therefore the term *separation anxiety* somehow downplays a condition.

Whether your puppy is fearful or anxious doesn't matter. What matters is they are feeling things they shouldn't—and that we can change.

The Facts about Puppy Separation Anxiety

Before we continue, we need to bust some myths about puppies and separation anxiety by setting out some facts:

- Puppies Do Get Separation Anxiety

- It's Not Your Fault

- Choosing a Certain Breed Is No Guarantee

- Letting Him Cry it Out Isn't the Answer

- Getting Your Puppy a Doggy Brother or Sister Won't Help

- He's Not Being Bad

- Puppies Do Go on Anxiety Medication

- You're Not Babying Your Puppy

Let's have a look at each of these.

Puppies Do Get Separation Anxiety

If you tell your friends and family that your puppy has anxiety, be prepared to be met with an eye roll. Thirty years ago no one was talking about anxiety in dogs, but as we become more aware of mental health in our own species (never more so than during the pandemic) we're more aware that we are not the only species that can suffer from emotional disorders.

As we have covered, puppies do get separation anxiety. Many arrive in their first home with fearful tendencies already present. Others develop them. So while we used to think that puppies didn't get real separation anxiety, and that any home-alone problem behaviors were just normal puppy stuff, we now know that they can and do get anxious when we leave.

It's Not Your Fault

Even if people don't say outright to you that you're at fault, they might hint at it. But your puppy's separation anxiety isn't your fault. Sure, there are things you can do to help prevent it, and things you can do to remedy it, but your puppy isn't freaking out when you leave because you're a bad owner or you are being too soft. Plenty of owners have multiple dogs, treat them no differently, and still end up with one dog having separation anxiety.

What do we know about the causes of separation anxiety?

We touched earlier on how genetics and life experiences play a part. But while we don't know exactly what causes any one puppy to be anxious, we do know some factors contribute, such as:

- Household changes,

- Changes in routine (COVID-19, anyone?),

- Moving home, and

- Being bought from a puppy mill or pet store.

But the data are far from conclusive. However, even though we don't know exactly why a puppy has separation anxiety, we luckily do know how to fix it.

Choosing a Certain Breed Is No Guarantee

It might seem like certain breeds are more prone to separation anxiety, but there's no concrete evidence to support this. But wait—aren't online separation anxiety support groups full of owners of breeds such as poodle-crosses, dachshunds, and French bulldogs? Surely that means these breeds are more prone?

It might seem that way, but that's because of the popularity of these breeds. If more people have these breeds, then it will seem like more of these dogs have separation anxiety. Our brain then calculates that this must equate to the chances of one of these breeds having separation anxiety being higher than for other breeds.

To truly understand the picture, you'd need what percentage of the population that breed makes up. We might assume that Chinese crested dogs aren't prone to separation anxiety because we rarely see them being discussed in forums. Actually if you went to any dog forum, you'd see it overrun by doodle and doxie owners.

If those same forums had existed in the 1970s, we might have said, "Afghan Hounds and Dalmatians are prone to separation anxiety," because of how popular these breeds were then.

All that said, I do think breed does have a role to play in

prevalence, but it's not breed genetics per se, it's breeding. When a breed becomes popular, good breeders can't suddenly turn on a tap that leads to a 400% increase in puppies. As a result, the demand is filled by less-experienced breeders and puppy mills. And we do know that puppies from puppy mills are more likely to develop fear-based issues, including separation anxiety. So maybe we are seeing more separation anxiety from certain breeds, but it has nothing to do with their breed. It's all about how they came into the world.

Letting Him Cry it Out Isn't the Answer

You didn't cause your puppy's separation anxiety, but here's one thing that can: letting your puppy have a scary time alone because someone told you it was just normal puppy behavior and that you needed to let him get on with it. Some people will tell you that if you come back while he's crying, you just reinforce the crying. In other words, he's now learned that if he wants you back, all he has to do is cry.

However, exposure to any experience at a level that's too intense can bring about fear. So a puppy who's not yet comfortable being left could develop full-blown fear of being left just by being exposed to a few sessions of "let him cry it out."

If your puppy is crying because he's scared, you must come back. It's easier to deal with a puppy who's learned that crying might get you back than one whose panic-based condition has worsened as a result of being left to get on with it.

The best option is not to go out for longer than your puppy can cope. That way you don't need to worry about coming back when he's barking, because he won't be barking in the first place.

Please ignore anyone who tells you to ignore your crying puppy. Chances are they aren't a specialist separation anxiety trainer.

Getting Your Puppy a Doggy Brother or Sister Won't Help

It can seem like the obvious answer, can't it? Your puppy struggles with being alone, so you need to get another dog or puppy. Unfortunately, for most puppies a companion dog doesn't cut it. They need human company. I've seen many people get a second dog only to find it has no impact on their current dog's anxiety, and studies support this.

Even worse, sometimes both dogs end up with separation anxiety!

He's Not Being Bad

I know it can seem like he's mad with you for leaving him, but he's not. He's frightened. That's why he barks, chews, soils (or whatever his problem home-alone behavior is). He's not doing it to get back at you. He's doing it as a cry for help.

Puppies Do Go on Anxiety Medication

I'm not a vet, so I can't advise you about putting your puppy on anxiety medication. Although you might have heard that puppies younger than six months can't go on anxiety medications, plenty of vet behaviorists do prescribe these medications for young puppies.

Always defer to your vet on matters related to medication. Just know that this could be an option for your puppy.

You're Not Babying Your Puppy

We're spending more money than ever on our dogs. We buy clothes, costumes, boots, beds, and endless varieties of treats, toys, and food. We give them their own social media accounts and share photos of their every move.

On top of that, we're moving away from training our dogs with fear and force. We make training fun and, instead of hurting or intimidating our dogs when they do something wrong, we train them to do something else instead.

As a result, keyboard warriors accuse us of "babying" our dogs. But is that really the case?

- Puppies are babies! They are needy and demanding. Meeting their needs is the right thing to do.

- It's only recently that we've decided animals should be treated with respect and dignity, and not tormented. With our puppies this means considering their needs and committing to providing a safe, warm, environment and keeping them well-fed, healthy, and free of fear. Being kind to them is not the same as babying them, though many old-school trainers think kindness is indulgent and permissive, which it is not.

- We used to think that human babies should be left to cry it out, but now we know that's not the right thing to do. It's the same with your puppy. If you decide that letting him cry for hours on end when you're out isn't the right thing to do, you aren't babying him. You're treating him with the respect he deserves as a sentient being.

- As a society, spending money is one of the ways we show love. You can buy items for your puppy without that meaning you think he's a human baby.

So no, you're not babying your puppy. You're caring for your puppy. That's all.

In a world in which we're overwhelmed with the volume of information available to us, and in which the repetition of a statement can make it seem like a fact, we need to get really good at separating fact from opinion.

How do we do that? Ask people how they know. When it comes to dog behavior and dog training, there's a wealth of research we can call on. When I hear someone declare, "This works," I want to know the source. I especially want to know the source if it's a new treatment that gets your hopes up and is going to hurt your wallet.

Here's a list of sources you can trust:

- Good-quality research studies on dogs (beware that not all research is created equally)

- Good-quality research studies on other species including humans

- The opinion of qualified professionals

Here's my list of unreliable sources:

- Just anyone on the internet

- Friends and family (unless they reference a quality source)

- Untrained or outdated dog trainers, especially those who rely on experience over continued professional development

Facts matter because, without them, not only might you end

up wasting time and money on things that don't help your puppy, you might also be advised to do things that could make him worse.

Is Your Puppy Worried about Being Home Alone because You Are Anxious?

You might be thinking, or have been told, that your anxiety is causing your puppy's anxiety.

Certainly, studies do show a correlation between a parent's neuroticism (a specific personality trait that is broader than anxiety alone) and separation anxiety disorder in children. Some studies do show that owners can contribute to their dog's anxiety. Dogs are very attuned to us. They can detect our emotions, and it does seem that they can get upset when we get upset. But dogs probably learn that when humans are upset, bad stuff can happen, or, at the very least, good stuff can stop. No wonder then they seem to stress when we do. It's usually not a good outcome for them.

However, none of the studies conducted on the link between owner and dog anxiety have shown that your feelings can cause your puppy to have home-alone anxiety.

Chapter Takeaways

🐾 Puppies can, and do, get separation anxiety.

🐾 You didn't cause your puppy's home-alone issues, but you can help him overcome them.

🐾 Puppy anxiety isn't a modern invention. It's real and your puppy may have been hardwired for anxiety.

🐾 Whether you're planning for a puppy, hoping to prevent separation anxiety, or looking to treat separation anxiety, the book has advice for you.

"

It takes as much energy to wish as it does to plan.

ELEANOR ROOSEVELT

CHAPTER 2

Planning for a Puppy

There's no doubt that planning for a puppy makes sense. By planning we can be more certain that we're getting the right puppy, at the right time, and with the right setup. When the pandemic was declared in March 2020 and lockdowns were announced around the world, many of us decided it was the perfect time to get that puppy we had always wished for.

76% (of the 900 people I surveyed) said their dogs were with them 24/7 during the height of the pandemic lockdowns.

58% of the people who got a dog during the pandemic said they'd been thinking about getting a dog for some time, but being in lockdown seemed like an ideal opportunity.

And it was an ideal time: We were home. We had time. We had very little else to do except bake sourdough bread and do online quizzes over Zoom.

But for many of us, getting a puppy had been a "someday" or a "maybe." We didn't have concrete plans in place.

If you got a puppy on a spur-of-the moment thing, and are now thinking, "Ugh, I feel so bad for not planning more," don't. Lockdown was strange and stressful. No wonder you wanted to welcome a puppy into your life.

Maybe you didn't follow the steps I outline to plan for a puppy. That does not mean all is lost. When I've had puppies in the past, I've not done all these things. I will, though, in the future. That's because I know so much more now about puppies, dogs, and separation anxiety.

If you are reading this with your puppy already at home with you, perhaps that could be your takeaway: that you'll come back to this book and go through the planning steps next time. There's plenty in the remaining chapters in this book to help you no matter where you are.

Meanwhile in this chapter we look at whether you can choose a puppy who won't get separation anxiety and talk about what factors to take into account when selecting the right puppy for your family and your life.

Then we move on to look at how to set up your home so you're all ready to welcome your puppy on day one.

This chapter also covers how to find a great trainer and what to look for in a daycare or pet sitter.

Before You Get Your Puppy

Is there a way to choose a puppy who is guaranteed not to get separation anxiety?

Unfortunately not.

However, while there are no certainties when it comes to selecting a puppy who won't get separation anxiety, there are things we can do to select puppies who will have a lesser chance of developing a fear of being left.

1. Be Wary When Picking Fashionable Breeds

If you have decided that you want a certain breed of dog, do be aware that puppy mills focus on producing puppies from the most in vogue breeds, especially when long-standing breeders are unable to meet the demand.

Good breeders have a limited number of litters every year and don't over-breed. Increasingly they are selecting their dogs for traits that make them good family companions. They aren't a production line. And while they are running a business, their goal isn't profit at all costs.

And that's when puppy mills or farms step in. They profit from breeding in-demand dogs and are motivated by their bottom line. The physical and emotional health of the dogs and the needs of your family don't factor in.

Research shows puppy mill dogs are more likely to suffer from fear-based problems and from PTSD. No wonder, given the start in life they have.

How can you spot a puppy mill? It can be tricky because puppy mills can be very sophisticated, but here are a few tips:

- Don't buy from an online advert. Good breeders have people applying to them. They don't need to advertise online.

- Visit the puppy at least once. See the puppy regularly from as soon as it's safe for them to have visitors. Or at the very least get regular updates from the breeder. Check the breeder's social media for video and photo updates.

- Don't be deceived by the offer to visit the puppy with its mum. We used to think that a surefire way to tell if you were getting a puppy mill dog was if the seller refused to let you see the puppy with its mum. Puppy mills are now wise to this. They fake it by arranging for the puppy to be available for you to see with an adult dog in a home with a human. But they won't offer that you meet the puppy regularly from an early age.

- Ask to meet both the mum and dad. The dad very often won't live with the breeder, but they will be able to put you in touch with the breeder who owns the dad.

- You could also look for breeders that start socialization early and raise the puppy in their home.

I'm not saying don't get a popular breed (hey, cockapoo mom here!). I'm just saying that you might need to be extra careful.

2. Find a Good Rescue

Puppies are much in demand at rescues. No wonder: Good rescues do an amazing job of making sure puppies get a great start in life, even if the puppy started out on the street.

If you're lucky enough to be selected by one of these rescues to be a puppy adopter, you'll get updates, be able to follow your puppy's progress on social media, and know that your puppy is getting the foundations he needs to be a well-rounded dog. There's no knowing what the puppy or his mum went through, of course, but notwithstanding that, a rescue puppy is a solid choice.

3. Consider an Adult Dog

Seriously! I know that might seem odd to read in a book about puppies. But you can do all the right things and still get a puppy who grows up into a dog who has separation anxiety. The only way to really be sure about how your dog will be when left is to get an adult dog who's known to be fine on their own. Even then, we know household changes can bring on separation anxiety, so there's still a risk.

Choosing Your Puppy

When choosing the right puppy, here are some key considerations to focus on. These include:

- The Full-Grown Dog's Size

- Coat

- Energy Levels

- Temperament

- Whether to Buy or Rescue

Let's go over each of these.

The Full-Grown Dog's Size

While petite people do get Great Danes, and men who are 6 feet, 4 inches tall pick chihuahuas, the size of the fully grown dog is something to take into account. If your dog gets sick and needs to be carried to the car for a trip to the vet, for example, are you strong enough to pick him up?

What if your puppy becomes so big and strong that he pulls like an ox on his leash? Do you feel equipped to handle that? If you have kids or grandkids, or if you have frail seniors in the family, a big, bouncy dog might not be the best choice for you.

Bigger dogs cost more to feed, and medication that is based on weight is more expensive. Some groomers also base the cost of the cut on the size of the dog. Even harnesses, collars, and dog coats cost more for bigger dogs. Sadly, bigger dogs also tend to have a shorter lifespan. If you live in an apartment or flat, there may be rules that limit the size of dog that you can have. Hotels often have a similar rule.

On the other hand, if you plan to spend your weekends hiking mountain passes or riding the trails with your dog, a bigger dog might be ideal for you. (However, plenty of small dogs can be up for this kind of adventuring.)

Ultimately the size of dog you pick is most likely to be based on your preference, but it is worth considering what size of dog will fit with you, your family, and your lifestyle.

Coat

Fluffy poodle crosses and other long-haired dogs (such as the Havanese, Portuguese water dog, or coton de Tulear) were increasing in popularity during the 2010s, and this trend seems set to continue during the 2020s.

Not only do many people find them irresistibly cute, but there's also a view that their coat is non-shedding, hypo-allergenic, and less likely to smell like full-on dog.

However, plenty of poodle crosses and other long-haired breeds do actually shed, and many dogs cause allergies. Plus, they are dogs and still have the capacity to smell like dog! Take it from me, mom of fluffballs: They don't always smell of sugar and spice and all things nice.

Those long, fluffy coats make them look adorable, but are prone to burs. The coats mat easily and need regular home brushing, and they need to be groomed regularly. Grooming visits aren't cheap, and lots of dogs end up hating them to boot.

On top of all that, when a fluffy dog gets muddy, you might as well dip a mop in sludge and wipe your floors with it.

There really is no such thing as a dog whose coat will not at least in some way cause a mess in your house.

That said, there's no doubt that golden retrievers will leave more of a trace than a short-haired dachshund.

But dogs are dogs, and they will make a mess of your house— or at least try to!

Energy Levels

If you pick a dog from a field or working line, you are opting for a dog who will need lots of exercise.

That said, most dogs could actually do with more exercise than they get. There isn't a breed of dog that doesn't need to be walked, played with, and given outlets for doggishness (you can read more about this in "Exercise and Enrichment" in Chapter 3).

Some dogs will cope with less exercise than they need,

whereas others will go stir crazy. Unless you can commit to giving your dog at least a couple of hours a day of off-leash exercise, stay clear of working or field line dogs.

Temperament

Breeds originated because dogs were needed to serve different purposes. That's why chow chows can be skittish with any person or thing they don't recognize (they were bred to guard) and why terriers like to dig and chew. It's also why Labradors can't resist water (and mud!). Do your research and consider a breed with a temperament that will be right for you.

Of course, if you rescue, you don't always know what you might get, and that's actually one of the joys of rescuing. You're usually getting a mixed breed (particularly if you adopt a puppy) and you might get a dog who has a temperament that is a mix of all the breeds.

Whether to Buy or Rescue

If you're set on getting a puppy rather than an adult dog, then your chances of adopting a rescue puppy are slim. Puppies are always in demand at rescues, and if you do find an adoptable puppy, you can be sure there will be stiff competition.

Rescuing a puppy rather than buying one means that you are contributing to a rescue organization rather than to a commercial operation, so if rescuing is something you want to pursue, don't be put off by the seeming lack of puppies.

It might take you longer and require harder work, but be tenacious.

Meeting Your Puppy

You've narrowed it down and have found a breeder or a rescue who has a litter of puppies. You're going to meet the litter for the first time to pick out the puppy.

What should you look for?

In the past we thought we could test puppies at an early age to predict the temperament they would have as adult dogs. However, research now shows that the predictive value of these tests is actually very limited. What does that mean? The tests don't tell us how a puppy will turn out as an adult.

The version of the temperament test that I used with India suggested a whole range of activities be carried out with a seven-week-old puppy. I opened an umbrella, I threw a rolled-up piece of paper, and I picked her up under her tummy to see if she would wriggle.

She passed all of these tests, but I have no idea how they impacted how she is today.

I didn't do them with Percy. I actually decided that because India was so easy I'd like a dog who would be more difficult.

The only thing I remember doing was picking him up under his tummy. *He squirmed!* It would actually take several years for Percy to be comfortable with being lifted up.

Breed characteristics aside, it's difficult to predict what temperament a puppy will grow up to have as an adult.

Training, socialization, and behavior modification can all have just as much impact on a puppy's personality as what happened to the puppy in the eight weeks before he comes home with you. So the personality of the puppy when you first meet them is not fixed. It may change as he develops.

██ Perhaps the hardest thing to change in a puppy is fear.

Perhaps the hardest thing to change in a puppy is fear. The fear that is most likely to cause problems for you and your family is fear of people.

All fears are tricky. When your puppy grows up into a dog who's frightened of having his body handled or who is frightened of other dogs, you have to make all sorts of accommodations. But a dog who is frightened of people will alter your life in more ways even than a dog who has separation anxiety.

That's why when choosing a puppy there's just one thing you need to look out for. Go for the puppy that runs up to you without hesitation. In fact, exploration is about the only test item that does seem predictive. The puppy who's curious and wants to explore will likely grow up to do the same.

Now, you might have read that the puppy who pushes to the front will be bold and over-confident, and that you'll end up with an uncontrollable dog who thinks he's boss.

This is nonsense. There's no such thing as an over-confident puppy.

Confidence is a good thing, and you can't have too much of it in a dog. The puppy who runs toward you is showing that he's emotionally healthy. Puppies younger than 12 weeks or so should be fascinated by people and show no fear.

The puppy who hangs back and looks wary is the puppy to avoid. Sadly, that poor puppy either has a genetic wariness of people, or he's had bad experiences in early life.

By all means pick the shy puppy if you want a project and/or if you're concerned that no one else will want him. But don't pick him thinking he's going to be an easy puppy who'll fit right into your family.

Setting Up Your Home

You've chosen a puppy and you have a date for him coming to live with you. Before you bring your puppy home, though, think about how to make your home a place that is safe for him. That also facilitates you managing his housetraining and his puppy chewing.

Here are the key decisions you need to make ahead of time.

Where Will He Sleep?

Allowing your puppy to sleep on your bed is not the catastrophe that old-school trainers would have us believe. It doesn't mean anything other than your puppy wants to snuggle, which is normal puppy behavior. So if you want him to sleep on your bed, do it. If you'd rather he didn't, that's fine, too.

You do want to make sure someone sleeps with him for at least first few nights. The shock of suddenly being alone in a cold kitchen, when he's been used to piling on top of littermates to sleep, will be hard on him. (See "Your Puppy Comes Home" in Chapter 3 and also "Nighttime Anxiety" in Chapter 6.)

Will You Try to Crate Train?

If so, get an appropriately sized crate. Crates that divide in the middle are ideal, as you can remove the divider as your puppy grows.

Which Parts of the House Will He Have Access To?

If you decide not to crate train, or if your puppy isn't comfortable in a crate, housetraining will go better if you think of your house in terms of puppy-proofed sections.

Puppy-proofing simply means preventing access to items that your puppy can chew on, or surfaces that will be hard to clean if he has an accident. If you live in an open-plan home you can create smaller areas by using exercise pens or extendible, freestanding baby gates/dog gates as barriers.

As more people seem to live in open-plan houses and apartments, there are more options for these items.

Will You Allow Your Puppy Upstairs?

If you've decided your puppy isn't going to sleep with you, you might decide that upstairs is out-of-bounds. If so, you need a baby gate or dog gate of some sort to keep him downstairs. Don't leave him to scream downstairs on his own, though. If you find you can't move around the house, try the Magic Mat plan that glues your puppy happily to his mat while you go about your chores. See the section in Chapter 4, "The Magic Mat Game" for more information on how to do this.

Who Will Be Involved in His Care?

It's important that your puppy has a variety of humans involved in his care. The more people he loves, the less likely he will be to become overly attached to you.

If you live alone get dog walkers, pet sitters, or friends and family involved in the fun stuff from day one.

If you live with family, stress the importance of them being involved, not just to lighten the load, but also, and more importantly, to make sure he grows up with lots of strong, yet stable attachments.

How to Choose a Trainer Your Family Can Trust

Finding a trainer you can trust for those important formative few months is vital.

It can be hard to know where to find the right trainer because, in most countries, dog training is an unregulated profession. What do I mean by "unregulated profession"? Think about doctors, dentists, lawyers, or vets. In most countries you can't call yourself a vet unless you have been accredited by the regulatory body for vets. Professional regulation exists to protect consumers like you. The goal is to ensure that you aren't given poor advice that could have adverse consequences for either your health, your safety, or your wallet.

However, anyone can call themselves a dog trainer without an education or a license. Marc Bekoff, professor emeritus of ecology and evolutionary biology at the University of Colorado, calls this dog training's "dirty little secret."

Why Qualifications Matter

I don't know about you, but I like professionals to be just that: professional. I wouldn't hire an electrician who wasn't certified. I'd take a dentist straight out of school over the one who learned dentistry at the "school of life." (Yikes!)

Yet somehow, we don't demand qualified dog trainers. We allow ill-trained individuals to advise families like yours about the pointy-toothed wolf descendant who lives in your home.

Depending on where you live, there are a number of different titles, qualifications, and letters after their name that dog trainers can acquire. This fact makes it very confusing when you're trying to choose a trainer.

Going by a title doesn't help either. You might think that someone who calls themselves a behaviorist or behavior consultant will know more than someone who calls themselves a trainer. Not necessarily.

Some people call themselves behaviorists and have no qualifications whatsoever.

Is experience alone ever enough?

Legally, experience alone *is* enough, because of the lack of regulation. However, experience isn't a standard. Years of experience don't tell you whether someone is doing something right. That might just tell you how long they've been practicing the wrong thing.

So how on earth do you choose a trainer? Here are three key principles to look for. They are:

- Transparent.

- Committed to Force-Free, Fear-Free Training—and Say So.

- Committed to Continually Updating Their Knowledge of the Science behind Dog Training.

They Are Transparent

A credible trainer will give you clear answers to any question you have. They should answer for you:

- What methods will you use to train my puppy?

- What will happen to my dog when he does something right?

- What will happen to him when he does something wrong?

You should hear that your puppy will be trained using food and positive reinforcement. In answer to "What if he gets something wrong?" you want to hear, "We'll keep showing him what we *do* want him to do and rewarding him for that."

If your trainer says they'll correct him, that's code for "We'll scare or scold him."

Don't believe a trainer who tells you prong collars, shock/e-collars, and leash-pops don't hurt your dog. They only work because they hurt.

And there's plenty of evidence that yelling at a dog might frighten them into stopping, but it causes ongoing fear and stress.

They Are Committed to Force-Free, Fear-Free Training—and Say So

You'll find that trainers who use force-free methods will talk about their methods. They have an explanation of their approach on their website. They may write blog posts about their commitment to force-free methods. They may share quotes, articles, or podcasts on science-based force-free training.

They are loud and proud.

They Are Committed to Continually Updating Their Knowledge of the Science behind Dog Training

Qualifications and courses taken aren't everything, but knowing that someone has invested their time and money into taking a course shows they care about being up-to-date. It shows their commitment to training dogs using the latest knowledge available.

If they are not the course-taking type, they will be into reading research, books, and blogs on science. You'll be able to tell this from their social media presence.

If you aren't sure how they keep up-to-date, ask them!

Beware of Dog Training Buzzwords

Force-free trainers are proud to tell you about the gentle yet highly effective methods they use. Trainers who use force know that we're all getting wary of being told to hurt or scare our dogs.

So they don't say they use force or fear. Instead, they say they are "balanced." *Balanced* is such a positive, non-threatening term, isn't it? Who doesn't want *balance*?

In the dog training world balanced means "I will use rewards, but I'll hurt and scare your puppy into doing what I want." It's a term they hide behind to avoid telling you what will really happen to your puppy.

It's a bit like saying, "I have a balanced parenting style. Sometimes I praise and reward my child. Other times I beat them."

Balance suggests a choice between two neutral options. Shall we use the blue harness or the red harness today? "Shall I reward my puppy or scare my puppy?" is not balance.

Beware also the use of these words:

- Leadership

- Dominance

- Corrections

All of these are code words for "trainer who will use fear-based and pain-based training methods."

Don't ever forget that you are the customer. It's your money and your puppy.

As Jean Donaldson of the Academy for Dog Trainers explains, "Demand to know what specific methods will be employed in what specific situations. Don't settle for smoke and mirrors."

If you don't get crystal-clear answers, or if something about the trainer doesn't seem right, don't hire them. Hiring a dog trainer is a big decision. Don't be afraid to be picky and shop around. As Marc Bekoff, leading dog expert, ethologist, and author, says, "Choose a dog trainer as carefully as you would a surgeon."

Rewards-Based Training

If you're like most puppy owners, you'll want to start teaching your puppy some basic behaviors and manners. Although I'd like you to prioritize home-alone training, socialization, and housetraining, I do recognize that you'll want your puppy to sit when asked, come when called, and walk nicely on leash rather than dragging you along.

If you are embarking on what some call obedience training and others call life skills or manners, then you need to use rewards-based training.

With rewards-based training, you reward your puppy for getting the right answer. Dogs who are used to rewards-based training know that it's worth trying to do what you ask because:

- Something amazing might happen if they get the right answer, and

- Nothing bad will happen if they get the wrong answer.

It's wonderful to see dogs who have been reward-trained react to a new training session. They respond with giddy excitement and anticipation!

What Do We Mean by "Rewards"?

A reward is simply anything that your puppy finds pleasurable. It's something that your puppy would like more of. What that might be varies by puppy but typically includes food, praise, play, and/ or belly rubs.

Food rewards are most frequently used in training because they are simple and quick to administer. For example, if I was teaching a puppy to sit using rewards, I could play a quick game of tug every time the puppy sat when asked. However, playing tug every single time will slow your training down and you won't get as many repetitions in a session.

With food, though, you can quickly reinforce the cued behavior with a small treat: behavior–treat–behavior–treat–behavior–treat, and so on.

Food is also highly motivating, of course.

But Isn't That Bribing Them?

Rewarding your puppy is no more a bribe than your wages are. We often ask dogs to do things that either don't come naturally to them or they don't want to do.

And that's why we pay them. Just as you expect to get paid for sitting at a desk all day long or being on endless Zoom calls, so you should expect to pay your puppy for things you ask them to do. Similarly, if you have kids you know how often you trade screen time for chores. Sure, sometimes kids will do a chore because they want to help out, but often some sort of negotiation takes place.

Maybe you think your dog should "just do it" to please you. I suspect, no matter how much you like your boss, you're not prepared to give up your salary and do your work just to please your boss. Dogs are no different in this respect. As much as they love us, they do need to be rewarded.

You might find some behaviors are so difficult for dogs that you have to pay them for life, even when they get better. Examples of difficult behaviors include recalling a dog with a strong prey drive away from squirrels or an excited greeter nailing a sit when visitors arrive.

Again, it doesn't matter how good you are at your job. You still expect to get paid. Dogs work for pay too.

The Benefits of Rewards-Based Training

There are various reasons why rewards-based training is the best training method for your puppy. Let's have a look.

1. **Rewards-based training is the ultimate in giving dogs choice.** They can choose not to do the behavior you've asked for. They can tell you when you've set the bar too high and it's stressing them. And they can choose to walk away when your training gets sloppy or you don't pay them fair wages for the work you've asked them to do.

2. **Dogs love it!** Why wouldn't they? They get access to things they love and get a tiny dopamine hit whenever they get a right answer. Plus, nothing scary or painful happens to them when they get an answer wrong. They really become addicted to rewards training—a beneficial

addiction. Don't be at all surprised to see your reward-trained puppy get excited when doing a new training session. In fact, I'd bet you'll respond with just as much joy, too!

3. **Humans love it.** Who wants to beat or shock their dog? Most people don't. With rewards-based training, the worst that can happen is your puppy doesn't get a treat (he will get over it) or gets a treat for the wrong behavior (not terminal). Rewards-based training is rewarding for us. It's easy to get kids involved, too. Simply hand them the treat bag. Imagine handing them a shock controller!

4. **Studies show that rewards-based training works better than force- or fear-based training.** On top of that, the side effect of fear-based training (training using shock collars, prong collars, alpha rolling, or anything the dog finds unpleasant or aversive) is the dog developing fear. For our sake and for the sake of our dogs, we should do everything we can to stop dogs from developing fear. We shouldn't train them with methods that are likely to create a lasting fearful response in our dog.

A big caveat: Here I am advocating for rewards-based training for your puppy, and yet, as you'll discover in this book, I don't recommend the use of rewards-based training for separation anxiety—and I especially discourage the use of food in training separation anxiety. I explain more in Chapter 4. For now, just know that rewards-based training is the way to go, just not for separation anxiety.

Choosing Care for Your Puppy or Adult Dog

Whether you go back to work immediately or whether you plan to take some time off, at some point you will probably be thinking about what to do with your puppy during the day.

Your goal might be for your grown dog to be alone for 10 hours or however long you're out of the house for work. We know that dogs do struggle—all dogs—when they don't have company. It's not that they go into panic mode; most dogs don't. Dogs do prefer company, though.

So if you think that, long term, your dog will be left the whole time you're at work, I urge you to rethink this. I'm not saying that you need to have your dog in daycare the whole day. For a start, not all dogs love daycare. But you do need to think about breaking up the day for your dog and especially for your puppy.

Your three main options are:

- Daycare,

- A pet sitter, and

- A dog walker.

When selecting any of these services, hours, location served, and price are all going to be important factors. Just as importantly, you need to consider training methods that the operation subscribes to. And if you suspect your puppy already has separation anxiety, consider what experience they have with dogs who have separation anxiety.

You want to ask:

- What training methods do you use? (Remember the list of "red flag" words that will tell you they use force and fear, such as *balanced, corrections*, and *leadership*.)

- What special measures do you have in place for puppies?

- Do you separate dogs by age and by size?

- What experience do you have with puppies and dogs who have separation anxiety?

With daycares and pet sitters, you also want to find out if they will let you have a look around and if they will accommodate you gradually getting your puppy used to coming to them by starting with short sessions of, say, an hour.

The best operators subscribe to force-free training (even though they aren't trainers they will be interacting with your dog, so this matters), have a low dog-to-staff ratio, and have a special process in place for puppies, small dogs, older dogs, and dogs who don't love to play with other dogs.

Additional Questions to Ask

Daycare

- What happens when staff aren't around?
- Do you crate puppies and dogs?
- If my dog can't be left alone, what can you do for him?

Pet Sitter

- What happens when you go out?

- My dog can't be alone. Can you assure that he won't be?

Dog Walker

- Can you guarantee that you'll always drop him off at the time we agreed?

- What happens if you drop him off only to find I'm not yet home?

Whether and When to Spay or Neuter Your Puppy

Let's close this chapter on planning for your puppy separation anxiety by covering a topic that's often hotly debated and that I frequently hear linked to separation anxiety: neutering your puppy.

The decision about whether and when to neuter your puppy is an important one, and it's one that you probably have been thinking about since the day you brought your puppy home.

In some parts of the world, neutering seems like a no-brainer. Typically in North America neutering is commonplace. In other parts of the world, keeping your dog intact is the more obvious choice. In some parts of Europe, for example, neutering is the exception, not the rule.

In the rescue world, neutering is almost automatic because of the desire to control population.

If you'd like your decision to be informed by evidence, then you might find it challenging to reach a conclusion from the available research. Different studies suggest pros and cons of spaying and neutering both in terms of behavior and health impacts. The evidence is always growing and changing, as are attitudes. In countries where spaying or neutering incidence has been high, questions are now being asked, in particular in an attempt to separate the need for population control versus the needs of the individual puppy.

To help you decide, I've set out two key considerations here. Be warned: There is no one answer that can be applied to all dogs. Arm yourself with as much evidence as possible and have an in-depth conversation with your vet about the decision for your puppy.

Health Impacts

A series of recent studies have looked at health outcomes in dogs neutered at or before six months versus neutered at or after six months. These studies focused on golden retrievers, Labrador retrievers, and German shepherds. What these studies tell us is that there are some risks of neutering in certain breeds—particularly that neutering increases the risk of disease that these breeds are predisposed to (in some instances). In some instances it seemed that early neutering was a factor, but that wasn't consistently found across all studies.

Earlier studies do, however, seem to show an increased risk of orthopedic issues in juvenile neutering.

Overall, most studies show that life expectancy is higher for neutered dogs. There seems to be consistency around neutering potentially increasing the risk of some cancers, while reducing the risk of others. For example, spayed females are less likely to develop mammary cancer, which is a common tumor (of which 50% are malignant) in female dogs. Spayed females are also less likely to develop less common and less deadly forms of cancer such as cervical, uterine, and ovarian cancers.

On the other hand, spayed females may be more predisposed to lymphoma and hemangiosarcoma.

When it comes to males, neutered males aren't at risk of developing testicular cancer, which is a common cancer, but they may be at more risk of developing prostate cancer, which is rarer.

You can see how the health benefits are complex to evaluate and why you need to discuss this with your vet.

Behavior Impacts

Equally complex is the impact on behavior. Until about 2018, studies seemed to suggest that neutering improved the behavior of male dogs in particular, especially with respect to marking, roaming, and inter-male aggression. However, more recently studies seem to suggest that neutered dogs are more prone to fear and aggression.

Is your head hurting yet? I did say it was complex. No simple, one-size-fits-all approach is likely to be optimal for everyone, whether it is early neutering, late neutering, keeping your dog intact, or using alternative approaches to preventing your dog from adding to the dog population (such as chemical castration).

Your best course of action is to make a decision for your puppy based on your puppy's individual needs, including the best age to neuter, which may be well beyond puppyhood.

Impact on Separation Anxiety

What stands out for me from all these studies though is that there is no strong evidence either way about the relationship between neutering and separation anxiety. Some studies suggest that intact males are more prone to howling and excessive vocalization when left; others show no such link.

I do regularly hear, however, people saying that their dog either started with separation anxiety or their separation anxiety worsened after neutering. I hate to be driven by anecdote and so am always wary to jump to conclusions just because the "evidence" seems so persuasive.

However, I do think that neutering could affect separation anxiety. It's not necessarily the hormone issue that concerns me, but the process itself. We know that dogs can easily develop fear (or develop worsened fear) as the result of just one event, if that event is significant enough.

Vet visits can be scary for lots of dogs and vet stays even more so. Consider the scenario of young dogs (even the typical upper age range for neutering is still only 18 months to two years) being hospitalized for the first time. They are away from their owner and their home, often crated, often isolated, and feeling pretty rotten. For a dog already prone to isolation distress, these conditions could well exacerbate the fear that being alone is not a good thing.

Can you see that the process itself might be the culprit here? Whether your dog is being hospitalized for neutering surgery or for another procedure, I recommend that you discuss with your vet how you can minimize the shock to your dog. In Chapter 4 I cover the process I recommend for vet stays. Review this process and ask your vet how best to accommodate your fearful dog during hospitalization.

It does pay to plan when you get a puppy. It's a big decision that will affect your family for many years. However, the pandemic turned the world upside down for all of us, so don't beat yourself up if you didn't plan as much as you would have liked.

In Chapter 3 we talk about the steps you can take once your puppy comes home that could help prevent separation anxiety.

Chapter Takeaways

- 🐾 Selecting a certain breed does not guarantee that your puppy will be free from separation anxiety.

- 🐾 A new puppy means lots of change for you and your family, so planning ahead helps make the transition for you and your puppy so much smoother.

- 🐾 Even if you got a puppy and weren't able to do the planning you would have liked, perhaps this chapter will help you think about what you might do differently next time.

- 🐾 It pays to consider how you'll set up your home to accommodate your puppy.

- 🐾 Choosing a trainer, pet sitter, or daycare in advance means that you're ready to get their support from day one.

"

The time to repair the roof is when the sun is shining.

JOHN F. KENNEDY

CHAPTER 3

Preventing Separation Anxiety

There are no certainties or guarantees when it comes to emotions and brain chemistry. Some puppies grow into adult dogs who develop all sorts of fears that we didn't anticipate. Others seem never to worry about a thing.

We can't predict.

However, if, during the formative weeks of a puppy's life, we give them good experiences and avoid them having bad experiences, then that gives us the best chance we have to prevent against fear.

When it comes to separation anxiety, this means teaching puppies how to handle alone time. And it means avoiding them having any bad experiences of being left.

Interestingly, we know that socialization generally is a factor in the development of separation anxiety (we cover this in "Why

Puppy Socialization Is a Vital Part of Home-Alone Training" later in this chapter). Some studies show that puppies who were never fully socialized are more prone to developing home-alone issues.

We might do all the right things with a puppy and they might still develop separation anxiety. But knowing that there are things that could help, and that might make a difference, we need to do whatever we can. Think of this sort of training like a vaccine: A vaccine doesn't guarantee that we won't get sick, but it does improve our chances.

That's why this chapter focuses on showing the steps to take so that you give you and your puppy the best possible odds of him not developing separation anxiety.

We cover advice on how to help your puppy settle in in the crucial first seven days at home. We explore why socialization matters and how you should approach socializing your puppy. I share fun and practical exercises that will show your puppy that this is his new permanent home and that when you leave you always come back.

We also look at how to set your puppy up for home-alone success with a gentle housetraining method that will prevent accidents when you're out. I take you through a crate training plan that gradually teaches your puppy to love his crate and show you how you can make your home puppy-proof whether you decide to crate or not.

Finally, we consider the role that exercise and enrichment play in preventing behavior problems.

Your Puppy Comes Home

At last, your puppy is home with you. The first day is exciting! It will be a memorable one so make sure your phone has plenty of space for photos!

So what now?

For most people the day-one priority is housetraining, and I agree you should focus on this (see the subsequent section "Housetraining"). However, you also want to put as much effort into getting him settled in the strange new environment he's just been dropped into. For example:

- Let him explore and sniff. Accompany him as he adventures around your home. Clear away anything he might get into and keep an eye on him in case he finds a new spot to pee.

- Throw some treats into the crate you plan to use (if you plan to do crate training). Allow him to find them. Keep popping treats in there throughout the day.

- If you have other pets, introduce him gently to them. Introducing puppies to cats could take up a chapter in this book so I recommend you read *The Trainable Cat*, by John Bradshaw and Sarah Ellis.

- Let him see his bed.

- Put some water for him in obvious places so he can find that.

- Play with him and do some hand feeding so that he starts to get happy vibes about you and his new home.

- You can even teach him his first behavior. Try sit or paw to impress the heck out of your friends.

On his first day home don't give him lots of alone time. For a start, he won't yet be crate trained, and there's a chance parts of your room might not be puppy-proofed. (See the later section in this chapter, "Puppy-Proofing a Space", for more information on how to do this.) But on top of that, he's in an alien environment that doesn't yet feel like home.

Give him the chance to see that his move is permanent. If you like you can play one or two games of puppy peekaboo (see the "How to Play Puppy Peekaboo" section in this chapter), but don't push him beyond this.

Make sure he has plenty of fun in the evening. Dogs by nature are active at dawn and dusk. (That's why puppies seem to go crazy at night and wake full of beans early in the morning.) Also ensure that he's had his last trip out to the toilet.

On the first night, I strongly suggest you sleep with him, either him in the room with you or you in another room with your puppy, say the living room. As we discuss in the section "Nighttime Anxiety" in Chapter 6, this arrangement doesn't have to be permanent. But that first night can be strange and scary for him. He's just starting to get to know you, but your home doesn't feel safe and permanent to him yet. If you disappear for the night, he'll be even more confused than when he arrived.

Observing Your Puppy

As a puppy parent, one of the most important skills to develop is reading your puppy's body language. Puppies and dogs send out lots of communication through their posture, their faces, and their movement.

Knowing what's normal for your puppy and what's not is vital. You can start this process as soon as he comes home. You'll be obsessing over him anyway so why not start to really observe him? For example, your puppy might naturally carry his tail high. Another puppy might have tail carriage that is lower—almost tucked. Often, we only monitor our dog's body language when they are stressed, so it can be hard to tell if a particular aspect of their body language is fear, anxiety, or stress, or whether that's just something they normally do.

The same is true for what some people call "displacement behaviors." These are behaviors that are normal, but that dogs might do with greater intensity when stressed or might do completely out of context: a dog suddenly deciding to groom in the middle of the park, or yawn when they're not tired, for example.

Often, when dogs do these out-of-context behaviors, people assume they are anxious or upset. However, if you start watching your puppy you might notice that they do have a habit of grooming at odd times and that they're not in an anxiety-inducing situation when they do it.

That's why I prefer the term *fidget behavior*. There's clearly some purpose to the behavior, but just as when we twirl our hair or nibble on a nail, this doesn't mean the behavior reflects a state of anxiety.

With all this in mind, I have an exercise for you. I want you to get really good at observing and recording your puppy's body language. I want you to pay attention to what they do in different contexts and not just when they might be upset.

Use the following table below to help you. (You can find a PDF copy of this in the resources page at www.berightbackthebook. com.)

What Your Puppy Is Doing	Your Observations (What body language do you see?)
PLAYING	
SLEEPING	
ENGAGING WITH OWNER	
GREETING	
DISENGAGING	
RELAXED	
ANXIOUS	

Getting really good at understanding your puppy's body language will help you enormously in the home-alone training.

Puppy-Proofing a Space

If you plan to leave your puppy for any period of time, you need to make sure he's safe and can't get into anything.

That's why you need to puppy-proof a room or a space in your house. Let's look at what that entails:

- Select a room that's large enough not to make him feel confined but that has the fewest puppy hazards (see the next point). The room should be one that he's used to spending time in, so don't pick the bathroom unless that's a room he associates with relaxing and happy times.

- Remove puppy hazards. These include (but are definitely not limited to):
  - Wires,
  - Fabrics,
  - Long curtains (tie them out of reach),
  - Loose floorboards,
  - Any objects on the floor or at puppy level,
  - Scatter cushions, and
  - Anything your puppy has shown an interest in chewing.

- Use extended baby gates or exercise pens to block furniture, countertops, or windowsills that you don't want him jumping up on.

- Remove or roll up rugs so he can't gnaw on those.

- Do fun stuff in the new space, such as rewards training or playing games. (If it's a room he already spends a lot of time in, you can skip this.)

This might all seem a bit of work, but safety matters, as does your peace of mind at knowing that your puppy can be left without worry. Now, remember: Just because you've proofed a room doesn't mean you can leave your puppy without going through the steps outlined later in this chapter (see "Practice Leaving Your Puppy") or if he's anxious being left. It just means that as you progress through the training and your absences increase, you don't have to worry about him getting into anything he shouldn't.

As we say in our house, if the dog got into something, we are the only ones to blame!

Why Puppy Socialization Is a Vital Part of Home-Alone Training

It might not seem like advice on puppy socialization belongs in a book on puppy separation anxiety. However, studies have shown that under-socialized puppies can be more prone to separation anxiety. That's why we're going to devote a whole section to socialization: I want to give you and your puppy the absolute best chance you've got to prevent home-alone issues.

Before you even brought your puppy home you probably heard the term *puppy socialization*. But what do we actually mean by that?

In order to unpack the process, we have to understand what goes on in your puppy's brain as it grows. Here are the stages of puppy development:

Stage	Characteristics
NEO-NATE TO TRANSITIONAL PERIOD (birth up to 3 weeks)	Puppies' eyes are closed. They can't yet walk. They are entirely dependent on mom and are not fully interacting with littermates. Their eyes start to open at the end of this period. They begin some movement around.
3 WEEKS TO 12 WEEKS	They stand up and start to move around. They play with their littermates. At about 6 weeks they can eat solid food. Puppies are curious about their world. Their brains are malleable and open to new experiences. • If they experience something new at this stage and that experience is positive, then they are less likely to develop fear of that in later life. • If, however, they experience something and that experience is scary, they risk having a fear of that for life. • If they don't experience something, there is also a risk that they develop a fear of whatever they don't experience.

Can you see how not learning how to be home alone *or* having a scary experience of being home alone early in life risks them developing a fear of being left?

However, beyond experiences of alone time, research shows that puppies who lack broader socialization also risk being more prone to separation anxiety.

Now, we don't know if this is causal—that is, did the lack of socialization cause the home-alone fear? It might be that puppies who weren't properly socialized were also more likely to be exposed to scary alone time during that impressionable stage.

// Getting your puppy comfortable with their world should be your priority for the first few weeks your puppy is home with you.

But the link seems clear, so we do want to make sure that puppies are properly socialized.

Regardless of whether this will affect them developing separation anxiety, puppies should be socialized. And getting your puppy comfortable with their world should be your priority for the first few weeks your puppy is home with you.

I know it can seem like teaching your puppy to sit or walk nicely on leash should be top of the list. However, your puppy has a lifetime to learn sit, but a crucial few weeks to learn that strangers aren't scary and that being home alone is safe.

If you're reading this thinking all is lost because your puppy is over 12 weeks, it isn't. We can continue to create positive experiences throughout our dogs' lives. It's just that those early weeks do carry weight.

Let's then look at what we can do in those crucial early weeks by way of socialization.

What Does Good Socialization Look Like?

Good socialization involves exposing your puppies to new experiences in a safe and non-threatening way.

What it Is

- Taking your puppy to a well-managed puppy class to play with other puppies his size.

- Introducing him to a variety of people, but not overwhelming him with crowds of people.

- Walking him on increasingly busy streets, starting with quieter ones and building up.

- Taking him for fun visits to the vet (bearing in mind that his first visit to the vet was most likely for a vaccination before you got him).

- Making a trip to the park with him, but hanging out on the edges or finding low-key, low-energy dogs for him to sniff and investigate.

- Letting him choose to approach strange things or new people—or allowing him to stand back and observe if that works better for him.

What it Is Not

- Taking him to the dog park and throwing him into the middle of a bunch of big, bouncy teenage dogs.

- When he's pinned by an adult dog saying, "It's okay. He has to learn." He does have to learn—that's true—but he doesn't need to learn that big dogs are scary because they roll him and pin him.

- Forcing him to be okay with anyone and everyone petting him even when he looks uncomfortable.

- Making him endure restraint or pinning for treatment at the vet so that he learns to get on with it. (He won't learn that. He'll just learn that being at the vet is rotten.)

- Dropping him into the middle of busy, crowded places instead of letting him observe.

- Saying, "It's okay. He has to learn." In the past we thought that being "taught a lesson" was a good thing. However, because of what we now know about how the brain develops, we know that those lessons need to be positive ones. We don't want him to learn that new things are scary. That's the opposite of what we're trying to teach him.

Lots of trainers will tell you that you need to expose your puppy to as many new experiences as possible during their sensitive period.

While this is true when it comes to socialization, quality matters more than quantity.

How to Socialize Properly

1. **Make a list of as many different life experiences your puppy might ever encounter.**
   You can start with the experiences in the Puppy

Socialization Tracker chart I've provided. Your list will differ depending on your lifestyle. For example, my dogs haven't been on public transport for years, but they see cross-country skiers at the dog park (that's rural Canada for you!). However, if I had a puppy now, I would try to tick off as many experiences as possible even if they weren't part of my puppy's life just in this moment. I would, therefore, look for an opportunity to take him on a bus because it might be part of his life in the future. You, however, might not need to seek out cross-country skiers! Remember: This is your one and only chance to socialize him, so you must be comprehensive.

2. **Expose your puppy to each experience in a safe, low-intensity way.** As your puppy goes through the experience, give him some amazing food, such as boiled chicken. That way not only does he think the new experience isn't scary, he'll also start to think it's pretty cool.

3. **Make the whole exercise choice-based.** Let your puppy tell you with his body language and his vocalizations whether he's okay with something or not. If he's not okay, back off from whatever is upsetting him.

Use this Puppy Socialization Tracker to record your puppy's socialization journey. Add your own ideas too in the blank spaces!

PUPPY SOCIALIZATION TRACKER

PEOPLE	# OF TIMES YOUR PUPPY HAS EXPERIENCED
Women	
Men	
Children	
Infants	
Teenagers	
Seniors	

PEOPLE WITH	# OF TIMES YOUR PUPPY HAS EXPERIENCED
Hats	
Glasses	
Beards	
Awkward gaits	
Physical differences	
Walking sticks	
Big coats	
Uniforms	
Overalls	

PEOPLE + ACTIVITIES	# OF TIMES YOUR PUPPY HAS EXPERIENCED
Kids playing	
Skateboards	
Adults on bikes	
Scooters	
Kids on bikes	
People playing football	
Picnickers	

AROUND TOWN	# OF TIMES YOUR PUPPY HAS EXPERIENCED
Busy streets	
School gates	
Vet office	
Groomer	
Pet store	
Train station	
Other people's houses	
Stores	
Dog-friendly restaurants	
The beach	

AT HOME	# OF TIMES YOUR PUPPY HAS EXPERIENCED
Vacuum cleaner	
Washing machine	
Broom	
Timer "bings"	
Lights switching on/off	
Dishwasher	

ANIMALS	# OF TIMES YOUR PUPPY HAS EXPERIENCED
Big dogs	
Small dogs	
Bold dogs	
Squirmy dogs	
Small puppies	
Big puppies	
Adolescent dogs	
Male intact dogs	

BODY HANDLING	# OF TIMES YOUR PUPPY HAS EXPERIENCED
Touching ears	
Putting drops in ears	
Looking at teeth	
Lifting tail	
Taking temperature	
Standing on scale in vet's office	
Filing/Dremel-ing nails	
Brushing	
Bathing	
Holding paws	
Touching body	
Patting head	

SURFACES	# OF TIMES YOUR PUPPY HAS EXPERIENCED
Grass	
Sand	
Concrete	
Carpet	
Stairs	
Floorboards	

SURFACES	# OF TIMES YOUR PUPPY HAS EXPERIENCED

SOUNDS	# OF TIMES YOUR PUPPY HAS EXPERIENCED
Microwaves	
Smoke alarms	
Car doors banging	
Thunder	
Fireworks	

VEHICLES	# OF TIMES YOUR PUPPY HAS EXPERIENCED
Your car	
Cars generally	
Motorcycles	
Scooters	
Trucks	
Coaches / buses	
Planes overhead	

You can download this tracker at www.berightbackthebook.com.

Use this tracker as is or expand on it to reflect your lifestyle and environment. Don't scrimp on socialization. Not only will it help you have a puppy who's carefree when he's out in the world, it's a foundational element to home-alone confidence too.

While you shouldn't overload your puppy on his first day home, there are items on the socialization list that you can tick off, even in his first few hours with you.

Your Puppy's Circle of Trust

As you work through your socialization list you'll look for opportunities for your puppy to meet with strangers. However, you also need to make sure that your puppy has a large group of familiar permanent people in his life. I call this your puppy's circle of trust.

This matters because some puppies can have the tendency to become overly attached to the one or two people who primarily care for him.

When this happens some puppies become distressed in the absence of their significant person or persons. Then, not only could this mean they struggle if alone, they can't be left with just anyone.

Therefore, when your puppy comes home think about who will be in his circle of trust. The circle could include:

- Your family,

- Friends,

- Sitters,

- Dog walkers,

- Daycare staff.

The more the merrier is ideal here. Get people involved in fun stuff such as feeding and playing with your puppy. And do what you can to ensure your puppy learns there is more to life than just you.

Why Puppies Don't Just "Know" We're Coming Back—and How to Teach Them

During research carried out in the mid-twentieth century Swiss psychologist Jean Piaget conducted various experiments to test whether children understood that just because something wasn't visible that didn't mean it ceased to exist.

Adults obviously have no issue with this. Just because we can't see something, we don't question whether it's still there—the cookie in the cookie jar, the car in the garage, our partner leaving the house to get groceries. We don't question their existence simply because they are out of sight.

Children seem mixed on this, though. For example, young children don't reach for out-of-sight objects. But they express surprise when objects disappear. As their brains develop, children learn that visibility and existence are not the same.

What about dogs, though? What do we know of their grasp of object permanence? Well, you know that you might put the treats away in the cupboard only to have your puppy sit at the cupboard door whining for them. But maybe your puppy smells the treats and that's why they know they're there.

Luckily some excellent studies have investigated what dogs do when objects disappear. A 2016 paper by Thomas Zentall and Kristina Pattison provides an excellent summary of the research. They conducted an experiment they called the "invisible displacement task." Here, an object is hidden and then moved away. The subject dogs are then watched to see where they go to look for the object. The idea is to test whether a dog remembers that an object is not visible.

We need to show puppies that things... that disappear haven't stopped existing.

A version of this test uses two buckets placed on either end of a plank. A researcher hides a treat in a container (so that the dog can't smell the treat) then puts the treat container in the bottom of one of the buckets on the plank.

The researcher then rotates the planks 180 degrees. This means that the bucket with the hidden treat has now switched to the other side of the dog. Most dogs will go to the side where the treat was originally hidden, which suggests dogs don't understand where the hidden object is.

However, this test is a bit skewed in that dogs will be drawn to the current location of the treat due to the logistical setup.

If the test is repeated, this time with one bucket near the dog and the other far away, we get different results. In this setup, the plank is rotated just 90 degrees, so the locations aren't competing. When this happens, the dog always heads to the bucket with the treat.

Two further versions of this test have the dog walking either 90 degrees or 180 degrees around the planks. When this happens, the dog heads to the right place to search.

So, these tests do seem to show that dogs have a good sense

of object permanence. That is, even though they can't see or smell the treat, it is still there.

But what about puppies?

While we don't have research into puppies' sense of object permanence, we do know that human babies aren't born with object permanence. They develop it at anywhere from between four and seven months.

Parents can help the development of object permanence by playing the simple game of peekaboo. Peekaboo might seem like a bit of fun; it certainly seems to amuse lots of infants and parents. In fact, development psychologists say the game of peekaboo has a much more important outcome: It helps babies understand that when something goes out of sight it doesn't stop existing. More significantly, it teaches infants that when their parent disappears out of sight they come back. People go and they come back. They go and they come back.

This early learning helps babies be better prepared when separation anxiety tendencies set in at later development stages.

Since dogs can learn object permanence, the peekaboo game can teach puppies the same valuable lesson: that you go and you come back. When a puppy first comes into your home, they have been separated from the family that they knew all their life up to that point. So for them, objects that have gone out of sight actually have disappeared.

That's why we need to show puppies that no, in this new world, things that disappear haven't stopped existing.

We do that with Puppy Peekaboo.

How to Play Puppy Peekaboo

1. Start with Objects

Take one of your puppy's favorite toys and hide it behind your back while your puppy watches. Then, rapidly bring the toy back into sight. Do this with a big smile on your face and with lots of fun, excited talk. You can even say, "Peekaboo!"

Repeat a handful of times, then play with your puppy and the toy.

Do this randomly and regularly with different toys. Or try doing it with treats, giving your puppy the treat on the last peekaboo.

2. Play with You as the Object

Pick spots where you can quickly disappear out of sight and return. Don't go far away. You just want to disappear for the briefest of moments. You could stand in an open doorway and simply bob behind the wall and back again.

Again, make it fun and silly.

If you find this stresses your puppy, don't disappear entirely. Stand behind the door frame and just have your head bobbing in and out of sight.

Then progress to all members of the household doing this.

Play the peekaboo game in different places at different times with different people. And start this on the day you bring your puppy home.

With human babies, it can help to start this with the parent being out of sight but still audible. I suggest the same with puppies, only "out of sight" is likely to mean still audible and within scent range, since we know how important scent is to dogs.

You're going to stay close enough that, even if your puppy can't see you, he can still smell you.

3. Progress to Puppy Hide-and-Seek

Hide-and-seek takes the game to a more challenging level. Make it easy to start with. Don't go too far from your puppy or hide somewhere he's not used to going. For example, don't hide in a cupboard in a room he doesn't usually have access to.

If he can't find you quickly, don't let him panic. Instead, call him and let the fun be him finding you by following your voice.

When he finds you, reward him with a fuss and a cuddle.

Gradually increase the difficulty: hide for longer, or in a spot that's more out of the way.

Keep increasing the difficulty of your hide-and-seek game, going slowly so as not to upset him.

Practice Leaving Your Puppy

If peekaboo teaches your puppy that when you disappear you still exist, practicing leaving teaches him that when go out you always come back.

Essentially, what we need to do is home-alone socialization. Remember that we said if we use socialization to expose puppies to novel items and situations while they are still young we stand a chance of them not developing a fearful response as they develop.

If they have a bad experience with the item or situation, they may develop a fear of it. Equally, if they have no experience of it, that too can cause fear to develop.

What we need to do, before a puppy develops a fear of being left, is expose him to alone time: Enough that he has adequate exposure but not so much that it scares him.

DESIRABLE	UNDESIRABLE	
Safe, manageable home-alone time	Scary alone time	Little or no alone time

The following plan is how you're going to do this. Note, this is different to the more involved remedial home-alone training that we cover later in Chapter 4, which is for puppies who are already scared of alone time. This plan is for confident puppies who aren't anxious when left but who just need to learn that you go out, that they will be alone at times, and that there's nothing to worry about.

Here's how to execute this plan

- Pick one or two of these steps a day.

- Leave through your main door, following the schedule in the table.

- If you need to put on a coat or shoes do so. Otherwise just go out as you are.

- Use a simple camera setup so that you can watch your puppy. (See "Set Up a Camera" in Chapter 4 for camera advice.)

- Once you get to five minutes you can try increasing the duration you're out by larger increments.

- Stop the exercise if your puppy gets distressed. Try again later.

Go out of the door for 30 seconds. Return.

Go out of the door for 60 seconds. Return.

Go out of the door for 2 minutes. Return.

Go out of the door for 3 minutes. Return.

Go out of the door for 4 minutes. Return.

Go out of the door for 5 minutes. Return.

REMEMBER

Only do one or two of these steps per day.

Stop if your puppy shows any signs of distress.

If stopping doesn't help and your puppy gets more upset by this plan, see Chapter 4 where we discuss home-alone training for anxious puppies.

Another excellent way to show your puppy that when you go you also come back, is to play the "Door is a Bore Game". See Chapter 4 for more information on how to do this.

Housetraining

Your puppy isn't going to be reliable to leave even for a minute without housetraining on board. That's why starting housetraining is obviously a top priority from day one.

In Chapter 1, we talked about house soiling when a dog is left alone as a key sign of separation anxiety. Remember that house soiling is only considered indicative if it happens when you are out and at no other times, and when it happens in a dog who is otherwise housetrained.

But, of course, your puppy hasn't yet learned where to go and that's why you need to start housetraining as soon as he's home.

A key part of this plan is preventing your puppy from having accidents. You can do this either by crating, since puppies don't like to soil their sleeping area, or by having him so close to you that you can watch him like a hawk.

You need to decide which approach you'll adopt. If you're not certain whether you want to crate, skip ahead to the section on crating in this chapter, where I set out the facts on crates.

If you decide not to crate you could try confinement, where you use an exercise pen to create a dedicated space for him where he has a little more space than in a crate.

Alternatively, you could use the approach I took with my own dogs. I housetrained all my puppies without a crate and it was pretty easy. I used gates and barriers to contain them in a smaller space *with me* rather than have them in a space separate from me. You could also use a leash attached to your waist if you can't watch him every minute or simply carry him around with you.

Okay, so on to the plan. You need the following:

- A crate only large enough for your puppy to lie down comfortably stretched out (or the ability to watch him like a hawk, as noted above), or a way of containing your puppy so that you can watch him, or a tether to keep him close to you,

- A schedule for going outside,

- Treats for whenever you go outside with your puppy,

- Good observing skills to prevent accidents, and

- Patience.

Step 1: Determine a Schedule

Provide your puppy with a set schedule for eating and for going outside. A typical puppy housetraining outing schedule looks like this:

- First thing in the morning.

- Whenever your puppy wakes from a nap.

- After each meal. This is often when puppies will have a bowel movement. You will discover your own puppy's rhythm.

- Depending on the puppy's age, every 30 to 90 minutes.

Step 2: Take Your Puppy Out according to the Schedule

Once you've determined your schedule, you are going take to him outside to toilet.

- Use the same spot each time so he begins to associate the area with its purpose. Don't interact with your puppy. Just let him get on with it.

- If nothing happens after five minutes, bring him back into the house and crate or contain him for 30 minutes. Then try again.

- If he does eliminate outside, give him a supervised free period in the kitchen or confinement area, or—better yet—a nice walk. This acts as a bonus for performing.

A very young puppy (six to eight weeks) may need to go out once during the night.

Step 3: Reward Generously

Every time your puppy eliminates outside, heap on the praise and produce a favorite treat. If the praise makes him stop in the middle of eliminating, save it until just after he finishes. Have treats and his leash ready near the door so you always have them to hand.

Step 4: Hone Your Observation Skills

Puppies give signals prior to eliminating. If you learn your puppy's signals, you'll catch far more would-be accidents before they happen. Common signal behaviors include circling, restlessness, and sniffing. Whenever you see these, take the puppy out!

Step 5: Don't Lose Your Cool

Most puppies will have accidents, especially in the beginning of training. Since your puppy will only be loose in the kitchen when he is "empty," mistakes will be seldom.

Supervise so you can take him out if you see him winding up. If you see him starting to eliminate, say, "Outside" in a bright, gentle tone and get your puppy there as quickly as possible. Don't shout at your puppy! Never punish, as this may inhibit your puppy from going in front of you. Punishment doesn't have to be physical. It could be a sharp word.

Stay outside for the five-minute period, and praise and give a treat if he finishes. If he doesn't go, bring him back inside and either supervise or crate him for another try later.

If your puppy has an accident in the house or in the crate and you did not see it happen, do not punish him. It won't work and it's cruel. Simply clean up the spot and apply a commercial odor neutralizer. Vow to supervise more closely in the future and/or add another trip outside to your schedule.

Points to Note about Housetraining

- If you are following the schedule and your puppy is still urinating several times an hour, take your puppy to the vet.

- If your puppy is four months or older and still having accidents, my guess would be that he has too much unsupervised, loose time in the house. Remember that each time he goes in the house, he is being de-trained and is learning that inside is the place to go.

- If your goal is for your puppy to go outside, paper training is unnecessary. It might seem more work initially to always have your puppy pee or poop outside, especially if you live in an apartment block in Canada and your puppy wants to go out at 10pm on a January night! In the long-run though, it's actually less work to train without paper. Train him to go on paper first and you're just putting off the inevitable work of having to train him to go outside.

To Crate or Not to Crate

Housetraining and crate training go hand in hand. It's easier to housetrain a puppy who you can crate. A crate can also keep a puppy away from dangerous cables or wooden table legs while you're out of sight, and so can be invaluable for making home-alone time safe. Crates can be incredibly useful for lots of other situations too, such as at groomer appointments or when you're traveling.

However, separation anxiety and crates don't go well together. In fact, even non-anxious puppies will need a gentle introduction to their crate. Never assume any puppy was born to love his crate. Even if he takes himself there voluntarily, there's a huge difference between him choosing to hang out in a crate and him having the crate door closed on him. Crate training will take work so decide if getting your puppy comfortable in his crate is a goal for you.

If you do decide to crate train, introduce your puppy to his new crate on his first day home. Make it a magical place where treats drop from the sky and food bowls appear from nowhere. He'll soon want to spend more and more time in this amazing place.

Puppies who don't have separation anxiety get accustomed to their crates quickly. They will whine to come out at times, but if they've had food and water, had a good play, and gone potty outside, and it's nap time, then you can ignore normal puppy whines.

Note that I'm not saying to ignore your howling puppy and leave him to cry for hours. I mean that non-anxious, short grumbles from your protesting puppy can be ignored. He's not anxious, and all his needs are met.

How can you tell a normal puppy whine from an anxious whine? The big differences are persistence and frequency. Protesting whines for a normal pup won't last long, and he won't always do them. There will be times—even on day one—when he'll toddle into his crate and be as happy as can be, even with the door closed.

This is key. If a puppy is anxious in his crate, he'll most likely display crate anxiety all the time. He'll be reluctant to go in there, and he'll take a lot longer to warm up to the idea of the door closing on him.

Crate Training Without Fear

This simple crate training plan will help your dog or puppy to love his crate. Note that I strongly recommend that you don't crate your anxious puppy when you are out.

You need to know that puppies who have had bad experiences in a crate require a lot of time (and a lot of your patience) to warm up to a crate. But it can be done. My dog Percy used to hate his crate. I worked this plan for six months until he would happily sleep in there at night. I still don't ever leave him in his crate when I go out, though.

And full confession: I gave up crating him at night two years ago, because I missed the snuggles!

What you need:

- A crate that's an appropriate size for your dog. (For more information on choosing a crate, visit www.berightbackthebook.com.),

- Yummy treats (lots of them!), and

- Tons of patience!

Be sure to follow these **"grading" rules**:

- Work in sets of five tries.

- If your puppy gets it right four or five times out of five, move to the next step.

- If your puppy gets it right three times out of five, repeat the current step.

- If your puppy gets it right one or two times out of five, drop to the previous step.

PHASE I
Getting Him Comfortable with Freely Entering the Crate

STEP #	WHAT YOU OR YOUR PUPPY NEED TO DO
1.	Randomly throughout day, drop treats at the back of the crate. • *Keep going for three days until he charges in as soon as he sees you open the crate.*
2.	Use a treat to lure him into crate, feed at the back (toss treat), let him exit at will. • *Move to step 3 when he does this five times in a row.*
3.	Lure him into crate and continue the flow of treats (~1 second apart) as long as he stays in crate. (Still let him exit freely.) • *Move to step 4 when he will stay in the crate happily for one minute.*
4.	Point to crate to hand-signal him into crate and continue the flow of treats (~1 second apart) as long as he stays in crate. (Let him exit at will.) • *Move to step 5 when he will stay in the crate happily for one minute.*
5.	Point to crate to hand-signal him into crate and feed and continue the flow of treats (~2 seconds apart) as long as he stays in crate. (Let him exit at will.) • *Move to step 6 when he will stay in the crate happily for one minute.*

PHASE II
Getting Him Comfortable with You Closing the Door

STEP #	WHAT YOU OR YOUR PUPPY NEED TO DO
6.	Hand-signal him into crate, move door to half-closed, feed, let him exit.
7.	Hand-signal him into crate, close door, feed, open door, let him exit.
8.	Hand-signal him into crate, close door for two seconds, feed, let him exit.
9.	Hand-signal him into crate, close door for three seconds, feed, let him exit.
10.	Hand-signal him into crate, close door for five seconds, feed, let him exit.
11.	Hand-signal him into crate, close door for 10 seconds, feed, let him exit.

PHASE III
Adding Duration

STEP #	WHAT YOU OR YOUR PUPPY NEED TO DO
12.	Make crate very comfy with bedding, hand-signal him into crate, give stuffed Kong or other special chew object, close door, hang out next to crate reading or watching TV for 10 minutes, dropping treats in every 20–30 seconds. • *Do this four to five times over two or more days.* • *Move to step 13 if he goes in without delay and displays no signs of distress when in there.*
13.	Repeat step 12 at a different time but now occasionally get up and leave room. Return within a few seconds. • *Do this four to five times over two or more days.* • *Move to step 14 if he goes in without delay and displays no signs of distress when in there.*
14.	Repeat step 12 at a different time but now for 30 minutes and feeding less frequently (every couple of minutes). • *Do this four to five times over two or more days.* • *From here you can increase duration as long as your puppy displays no signs of distress when in the crate.*

Facts about Crating

There are few, if any, aspects of separation anxiety that create more mythology. To clear things up I want to provide some facts on this topic.

Crating Doesn't Fix Separation Anxiety

We used to think that crating a dog would help home-alone anxiety. But here's the thing: Many dogs who have separation anxiety also have a phobia of crates. For these dogs, crating adds to their panic.

Do we know why crate phobia and separation anxiety seem to go hand in hand? Not really, though if I had to guess I'd say the crate might add an extra level of isolation for a dog who already feels scared when alone.

Or maybe a dog who has separation anxiety has just spent too many long absences in his crate and has come to associate the crate with scary alone time.

Yet, if you have a dog who's chewing the walls or ripping up the floorboards, a crate can feel like the only answer. It does stop the damage to your house, but you risk severe physical and psychological damage to your dog. Panicking dogs will harm themselves trying to escape. The memory of the panic is lasting.

I'm not anti-crate—far from it. Crates are invaluable tools for containing excitable dogs who try to knock over visitors or for confining dogs while at the vet or the groomer. And they are wonderful tools for housetraining. That's why I devote a section in this book to crate training.

To an anxious dog, though, a crate is not a safe haven. It's a punishment.

Just Because Dogs Seem to Like to Den Doesn't Mean They'll See the Crate as Their Safe Space

Because we see wolves denning, we've made the leap that dogs do too, and that the den they would choose is a closed crate. It certainly seems that dogs like a den-like setup to nap in. And dogs who are frightened of thunder or fireworks will often choose to huddle in a crate.

However, there's a big difference between denning and crating: the door. Dens don't have doors. Dogs are free to enter and exit. With crates however, we think that by closing dogs into a crate they will feel safer. For many dogs the opposite is true, especially if we haven't gone through the fear-free crate training plan (and sometimes even if we have).

Thunder-phobic dogs might like to hide in their crate, but they can freak if they aren't free to exit. The same is true with dogs who are frightened of alone time or confinement.

If you want to make his crate into a safe space for when you leave, do it. Just leave the door open and let him choose whether he wants to enter and whether it really does feel safe in there.

Him Being Okay in His Crate at Night Doesn't Mean He'll Be Okay When You Leave

You might be feeling confused as to why your puppy seems fine in his crate at night, but as soon as you crate him when you try to leave, he loses it. This is a common scenario. For whatever reason, some puppies decide they are okay in their crate in a certain context but not in another. It makes sense in his head!

If getting him comfortable in his crate at all times is your goal, take comfort from the fact that he's shown he can be okay in his crate in one context. He just needs to use that crate confidence in other contexts.

"Anxiety Crates" Aren't the Answer

You may have seen crates that promise to fix separation anxiety because they are constructed such that the dog or puppy cannot escape. These supposedly indestructible crates may be just that—but puppies still manage to injure themselves. And even if there's no physical harm done, the neurological damage done by locking a panicking puppy in a cell-like crate may be irreversible.

You Can Housetrain without a Crate

As I explained in the earlier section in this chapter "Housetraining," you can housetrain without using a crate. In many countries in the world (Scandinavian countries, for example) crates are rarely used, and yet owners there housetrain puppies without issue. You just need to take a different approach.

You Don't *Have* to Crate Your Puppy to Prevent Destruction

You might wonder how on earth you can trust your puppy when you leave if you don't use a crate. First, you can set up a puppy-proofed area. (See "Puppy-Proofing a Space" earlier in this chapter.) Second, if your puppy is chewing or soiling because he's upset, then not leaving him for longer than he can handle will stop this. Third, if you're doing home-alone training (see "Gradual Exposure Training Steps Explained" in Chapter 4) you'll be watching his every move on camera, so you'll be back way before he has chance to get up to anything.

> Training is important in preventing home-alone issues, but training alone isn't the solution.

You Can Do Separation Anxiety Training with Your Puppy in a Crate–but It's A Lot More Work

If crate training just isn't working out for you and you keep getting stuck (step 12 of the crate training plan seems to be the biggest stumbling block for most puppies), then don't do it. It really isn't essential. But if you are determined to get him to be happy in his crate when you leave, continue on. Just know that it will take more time and require more effort.

Exercise and Enrichment

Training is important in preventing home-alone issues, but training alone isn't the solution. Exercise and enrichment are vital components in preventing emotional issues in puppies.

Those of us who lived through pandemic lockdowns know all too well how mental well-being can suffer when we are deprived of exercise and aren't able to enjoy our usual pastimes.

Feeding our puppies and keeping them warm and away from

harm aren't enough. They have other needs that we need to make sure we meet.

Let's look at those needs starting first with exercise.

Exercise and Puppies: Facts First

From what I've read, many owners and trainers seem to have hard and fast rules about how much exercise puppies should have. These opinions, though passed off as fact, lack solid scientific evidence to support them.

It might surprise you to learn that the recommendation of "one minute's exercise for every week of age" is not based on anything concrete.

In fact, very little is known about the risks or the benefits of exercise for puppies. In particular, studies don't indicate how much, what type, or what intensity is best for puppies.

Two studies suggested that playing with other dogs or chasing balls or sticks did seem to be a risk factor for the development of joint problems. However, neither answered the questions of how much and what intensity, nor did they study the benefits of exercise, which there undoubtedly are, including helping prevent some forms of joint abnormality, keeping obesity in check, and just being normal, necessary, and enriching puppy behavior.

While the studies into puppies are limited, there are more studies on children. Veterinary scientists are cautious about basing canine advice on human studies, but vet Dr. Brennen McKenzie says:

> [T]hough it is always risky to extrapolate from
> one species to another, some useful information
> can be gained by using one organism as a model
> for another, as long as conclusions drawn in this

way are cautious and tentative pending better data. In general, while some intense and repetitive exercise can pose a risk of damage to growth plates in children, exercise is overall seen as beneficial in improving bone density and reducing the risk of obesity and related health problems.

We really don't have conclusive advice regarding puppies and exercise, but we *can* be sure that the received wisdom to severely restrict puppy exercise isn't actually the evidence-based advice we might think.

Myths in training and dog care trouble me deeply, and they are often made more "fact-like" when they are repeated, without question, on the internet.

I'm not a vet, so I can't give medical advice. What I can tell you, though, is that *in my opinion,* based on the research I've read, we don't need to be as restrictive with puppy exercise as some people would say. General principles about avoiding forced exercise or overdoing voluntary exercise seem reasonable, and we do need to be careful with puppies around the home: on stairs, on slippery floors, and when jumping in and out of cars, and on and off beds.

But if you're getting advice, especially from non-medical specialists, that a certain type of activity, a particular surface, or a length of time can present risks to your puppy, ask where they got their data. Chances are it's based on the opinion of someone posting online. Opinions are fine, but people really should disclose when they are basing advice on opinion rather than fact.

If in doubt, ask your vet or your canine physiotherapist (my go-to for questions about my senior dogs and their exercise).

Whatever you do, don't sequester your puppy. Access to the

great outdoors is highly stimulating and great for their developing brains. Like humans during lockdown, puppies and dogs can go stir-crazy if they don't get outside.

Enrichment: What Is it and Why Does it Matter?

Enrichment is allowing your puppy an outlet for his natural behaviors. Studies carried out that look into the behavior of zoo animals show that these animals become stressed if they don't have an outlet for their natural behaviors. In some captive animals this can even develop into what is called zoochosis, a form of psychosis.

Enrichment, first and foremost, is about giving animals an opportunity to express their natural tendencies. For dogs, natural behaviors include:

- Chewing.
- Dissecting.
- Hunting.
- Chasing.
- Sniffing.
- Running.

Allowing dogs to take part in any of these activities provides both a mental and a physical workout. These activities aren't just important to adult dogs: They matter to puppies too.

Look for ways to build more enrichment into your puppy's day, focusing on whichever natural behavior your puppy loves most. Exercise, games, nose work, and puzzle feeders are the obvious ones, but conjure up other opportunities: trips to the store, having people around, having friends take your puppy out, brain games, rewards training—the list is long.

Socialization, when done properly, is actually a fantastic form of enrichment!

Rewards-based training is another great way to engage with your puppy and provide mental stimulation. If you train with a plan, are clear about what you expect your puppy to do, and use tasty rewards, training becomes a fun, enriching activity. It's all tricks to dogs, but trick training is fun for everyone (kids love it!) and is a super way to teach impulse control, which is an invaluable skill for puppies to learn.

Choice also adds to enrichment. Give puppies choice over who they want to play with, which strangers they are happy to have pet them, which toy they want to play with, and even which treat they want to train with today. And let them say "no."

Don't think about enrichment as yet another thing to do. Sure, do get puzzle feeders and play games with him, but don't overlook more organic ways to spice up his life.

Enrichment Tips

As with exercise, we can sometimes get caught up in thinking that too much enrichment is a bad thing. You might also worry about articles you've read that too much excitement will result in a puppy who will never be able to settle on his own.

Let's have a look then at some enrichment tips for your puppy.

Don't Worry whether He's Getting Too Much Enrichment; Worry whether He's Getting Enough

When it comes to dogs, most suffer from lack of enrichment, not too much, yet I often hear the charge "Enrichment activities make things worse for dogs." For example, I hear that "fetch-heads" are more stressed by a game of ball than by not playing ball. There is no evidence to back this up. The limited research on the topic is inconclusive.

Saying that a puppy is getting too much enrichment is like us saying "I've taken too many beautiful walks in nature" or "I've spent too much quality time with my family." Enrichment makes us feel better, not worse. If an enriching activity is addictive, it's addictive in a good way.

We do know zoo animals have more behavioral and health issues when they don't get to express the species-specific stuff they were born to do. Most vets and trainers would say the same about dogs. Few, if any, pet dogs are going to suffer from too much enrichment. If they did, I'd put that in the category of "nice problem to have."

Is it possible for the thing you love to do to also stress you out? Of course. Anyone who's ever followed their team in a major competition will tell you the win/lose anxiety is real. But that's the whole point: The adrenaline rush that comes from nail-biting games is why we love sports.

In his bestselling book on stress, *Why Zebras Don't Get Ulcers*, Robert Sapolsky gives a helpful explanation of adrenaline junkies. He explores the reasons why long-term exposure to stress is harmful, and contrasts this with how short-term stress is beneficial and increases dopamine. That's why we like nail-biting sports games and why dogs love fetch.

Sure, these short-term rushes can become addictive, but for some, not most. If you're worried, mix it up for your puppy.

In fact, variety is as important as control when it comes to the mental health of zoo animals. So, for your puppy, mix up time, location, game, whatever—but don't deny your puppy. The harm of not giving him an outlet for his chase needs outweighs the risks.

Accept that Animal Planet Plays Out in Your Living Room

Is our need to have well-behaved dogs impacting their welfare? Is it possible to mold these pointy-toothed creatures without trampling on their needs?

Yes, it is. We can have a well-behaved dog who also gets to be a dog. We need to do a bit more accepting and a bit less suppressing. Remember that many of the things we're asking them to stop are normal dog behaviors—dogs being dogs. I'm not suggesting you let them run wild. Sometimes let them be more dog, that's all.

Just Because a Behavior Stresses Us, Don't Assume it Stresses the Puppy

There seems to be much chatter about overexcited puppies. Puppies who jump, run, zoomie, chase, or engage in whatever puppy-like activity cause concern for some. Somehow an idea has taken hold that doing nothing is the best way for puppies —and dogs—to avoid anxiety.

But is the anxiety ours? Maybe we're the ones stressed, by full-on "dogs just being dogs."

Zoomies, or those frenzied moments when dogs tear around seemingly out of control, top the list of contentious behaviors. As with fetch, there is no evidence zoomies are causing anxious dogs. And dogs love to zoom. Marc Bekoff, dog writer and professor of ethology, says, "If they didn't [love zoomies], it's highly likely they wouldn't engage in them. Zoomies are surely part of what it's like to be a dog."

There's a good chance that the physical, frantic exercise we see our dogs do is releasing beneficial hormones, such as dopamine and serotonin, and removing unwanted ones, such as cortisol and epinephrine, from their systems. Studies certainly show this is the case for humans, as a 2020 article by the American Psychological Association explains: "Research shows that while exercise initially spikes the stress response in the body, people experience lower levels of hormones like cortisol and epinephrine after bouts of physical activity." Don't deny your puppy fun just because it seems too full-on or you might be denying him a way to get rid of stress hormones.

Find What Helps Your Puppy Relieve His Stress

You might have heard of the stress bucket concept—that dogs, like we humans, have a limit to how much stress they can take before they melt down. While it is a helpful concept, we need to remember what *empties* the stress bucket. Your puppy might have had a scary trip to the vet and bad encounter with a bigger dog at the park. That might leave you feeling that his stress bucket is full.

But despite internet advice to the contrary, the way to empty his stress bucket is not to lock him in the house for three days, limiting his exposure to the world and to social interactions with his species.

What does empty his stress bucket will depend on him. For the puppy who is frightened by life, laying low for a few days could be beneficial.

But if there's one thing we've learned during the pandemic, staying home and not exercising, not doing the things we love, and not having social interaction, are ruinous to our mental health. It's the same for puppies.

Every puppy has a different-sized stress bucket. All the things we've talked about, such as early life experiences and socialization, increase the size of the puppy's stress bucket. Not only that, but these puppies tend to have leakier buckets. Their buckets empty quicker. Another term for all of this is *resilience*.

Don't assume that just because your puppy has had a bad day, he needs to stay home. Let him have some fun and see how quickly he bounces back. It's time we stopped locking down dogs and instead let them be more dog.

Let Them Be More Dog

Modern domestication is failing our dogs. Fed and sheltered aren't enough. However, we can remedy this. There are so many easy and cheap enrichment solutions. The biggest cost is usually our time, but we must invest.

If our dogs could talk, they'd tell us how grateful they are for what we do give them. But, they'd add, could we let them be a little more dog?

Bringing it All Together: Your Puppy's First Week Separation Anxiety Proofing Plan

In your puppy's first week with you, not only do you need to teach your puppy that people leave but they always come back and that being alone is safe, but you also want to teach him that this new place is his permanent home.

You'll want to try a few basic obedience behaviors, too.

And of course, you need to start housetraining and work on crating if you're going to use a crate for your puppy.

On top of all that, you won't want to delay socializing him.

That's a lot! I've created this seven-day plan so you're clear on what you need to do and so you have a structure to guide you.

I recommend planning for someone to be with your puppy for the first week. You don't have to pay for fancy sitters or daycare. Plenty of people will happily spend time with a squidgy new puppy! When mine were babies, my niece brought her books with her and did her university studies while hanging with my puppies. It was rough for her, as you can imagine.

The following tables outline what you need to do during that crucial first week to help your puppy gain home-alone confidence.

DAY ONE

Your first full day with your adorable puppy! You're getting to know each other. Today your puppy will begin to learn:

- *He's here to stay.*
- *This new place is permanent.*
- *You might come and go, but you always come back.*

TODAY'S ACTIVITIES

Low-key Puppy Peekaboo exercises. *

Door is a Bore. Start with door touches. *

Housetraining.

Have your puppy sleep next to you when you sleep.

* Do both of these when your puppy is sleepy, full, and empty, and the action is over. See SAFE rules on "What's Normal Puppy Behavior and What's Separation Anxiety?" in Chapter 1.

DAY TWO

TODAY'S ACTIVITIES

Low-key Puppy Peekaboo exercises.

Door is a Bore. See how many steps you can get through.

If you've decided to crate train start with step 1.

Tick at least 2 or 3 items from Socialization Tracker. *

Housetraining.

Teach him to sit.

Have your puppy sleep next to you when you sleep.

* See the section on socialization earlier in this chapter for a list you can use.

DAY THREE

TODAY'S ACTIVITIES

- Low-key Puppy Peekaboo exercises.

- Door is a Bore. See how many steps you can get through.

- Continue crate training.

- Tick at least 2 or 3 items from Socialization Tracker.

- Housetraining.

- Teach him to shake a paw.

- If you don't want him to sleep on your bed, try to have him sleep in the location you've chosen for him.*

* See the section "Nighttime Anxiety" in Chapter 6 if he struggles with sleeping away from you.

DAY FOUR

TODAY'S ACTIVITIES

- Low-key Puppy Peekaboo exercises.

- Door is a Bore. See if you can get to the last step.

- Continue crate training.*

- Tick at least 2 or 3 items from Socialization Tracker.

- Housetraining.

- Teach him to spin.

* If you find crate training isn't working, take a break and consider housetraining without a crate.

DAY FIVE

TODAY'S ACTIVITIES

- Continue crate training (if you're still committed to that).

- Housetraining.

- Tick at least 2 or 3 items from Socialization Tracker.

- Do random Puppy Peekaboo throughout the day.

- Work on one of the behaviors from days 2-4 to strengthen the learning.

DAY SIX

TODAY'S ACTIVITIES

- Start practicing leaving using the plan in the section "Practice Leaving Your Puppy" earlier in this chapter.

- Continue crate training.

- Housetraining.

- Tick at least 2 or 3 items from your Socialization Tracker.

- Do random Puppy Peekaboos.

DAY SEVEN

TODAY'S ACTIVITIES

- Continue home-alone training.*

- Continue crate training.

- Housetraining.

- Tick at least 2 or 3 items from your Socialization Tracker.

- Do random Puppy Peekaboos.

* If your puppy is struggling, go to Chapter 4 ("Gradual Exposure Training Steps Explained") to read more about how to help a puppy who is anxious being left. This could be your puppy.

Chapter Takeaways

- We can't ever guarantee that puppies won't develop separation anxiety, but that doesn't mean that we can't try.

- We do know that some things do make a difference to a puppy's prospects for being happy when home alone. These include socialization, puppy home-alone training, and not leaving your puppy to get upset.

- You'll have a lot going on in the first seven days that your puppy is home. Following the plan that I outlined in this chapter will help you keep on top of everything you need to do.

- Housetraining is probably your top priority but make sure that home-alone training is high on your list too.

- Puppies don't always love being closed in a crate. Many need patience and gentle training to help them learn to love their crate.

- Since we know how important socialization is to helping your puppy be home alone, start this as soon as you can.

- Exercise and enrichment have a big impact on your puppy's emotional well-being, so make sure you find ways to keep his life fun and stimulating.

"

The best time to plant an acorn is 20 years ago. The second best time is today.

CHINESE PROVERB

CHAPTER 4

Treating Puppy Separation Anxiety

What if, despite all the planning and taking every preventative measure possible, your puppy still gets anxious when left? Or what if you didn't know about all these things and were given bad advice? The good news is it's not too late to teach your puppy to be happy at home alone. That's what this chapter is all about.

Separation anxiety is a phobia. It's a phobia just like the phobias people get. Maybe you're afraid of heights or you don't like spiders. For a dog who has separation anxiety, the phobia is the fear of being alone. We train separation anxiety—the way that we get the dog over it—by using the same therapy used to treat human phobias: gradual exposure to the thing that causes the panic.

Once you realize that your puppy fussing when you leave is more than just normal puppy stuff, you'll want to use this method to teach him that being home alone is safe.

Gradual Exposure to the Scary Thing

When we gradually get over a fear, we are using a process that in dog training we call *desensitization*.

Whenever we want to get a dog more comfortable with something he's scared of—be that strangers, nail trimming, or noises—we take a tiny dose of the thing that scares the dog, but at a low, non-frightening intensity, and then gradually increase the intensity at a pace the dog is happy with.

Take nail trimming, for example. We might start by just showing the nail clippers to the dog. Then, when the dog seems fine with that, and shows no fear, we might bring the clipper toward the nail. Then we might touch the dog's nail, and so on.

With separation anxiety training, we expose your puppy to the amount of alone time that he can cope with at any one time. We gradually increase that alone time as the puppy learns that being on his own for that amount of time is safe. And we keep adding time to that duration—as long as your puppy is comfortable.

The key is that the intensity of each step must never be too much for the puppy. Your puppy needs to feel at every step that he's okay and there's nothing to be frightened of.

That's separation anxiety training in a nutshell.

Training Thresholds Explained

Critical to successful training is keeping your puppy under his anxiety threshold. We go at your puppy's pace.

We let him tell us what he's comfortable with and how much more he could do. We never let him go over what we call his anxiety threshold (the point at which the puppy crosses over from coping to freaking out in panic at being left alone).

If the puppy does go over his anxiety threshold then he will not feel safe. Now, we are not reprogramming him to think that being on his own is fine.

An anxiety threshold is the imaginary line of your ability to tolerate stress, anxiety, and new situations at any given time. Thresholds are at the heart of separation anxiety training. We need to understand our puppy's thresholds if we are to get a puppy over his anxiety.

The following diagram shows three different levels of threshold:

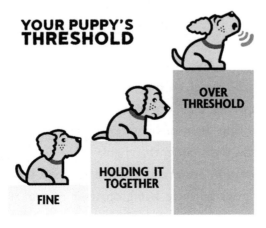

The puppy on the bottom step is happy and relaxed, and doesn't perceive anything threatening or scary. A dog who is okay on his own at home will always be in the "Fine" section of the diagram. We call this *threat unaware*. He isn't scared and doesn't feel threatened when left home alone.

As your puppy starts to perceive that something isn't right he becomes *threat aware* ("Holding it Together" in the diagram). When you work on separation anxiety, you need to catch your puppy if he's heading toward that threat-aware zone. You don't want him to enter the next zone, in which he's gone beyond just being aware of the threat and is now in full-blown flight, fight, or freeze response to that threat.

Let's think about an example of thresholds in another context. Imagine a zebra grazing on the savanna, blissfully unaware of anything bad going on in his world. We call this threat unaware.

He then sees a lion on the horizon. That starts to trouble him. He is now most definitely threat aware. His anxiety level has increased, and all of the biological symptoms of increased anxiety have also kicked in.

At this point the zebra must decide: Does he need to seriously worry about that lion? Or is that lion so far away that it's not a problem?

When the zebra decides that the lion is truly a threat, he tips into the third zone. Now he's not only threat aware, but he's responding to the threat. He thinks that the lion has spotted lunch, and the zebra wants to get out of there as quickly as possible. He's in full-on panicking, flight-or-fight mode. The zebra, being a zebra, most likely picks flight rather than fight!

With separation anxiety, the threat is alone time. We have no idea why dogs perceive being on their own in this way. To

us, it seems totally irrational. Having seen
hundreds of panicking home-alone dogs
there's no doubt in my mind that, to these
an existential threat.

Learning about Your Puppy ⸺ Threshold

When your puppy goes over threshold, you add another bad
episode to his anxiety bank. Very quickly, it can start to feel
like you will never get out of the red. That is why learning and
understanding your puppy's threshold tolerance are so critical
when training an anxious puppy.

To show your puppy that you leaving him for a few hours isn't
scary, we need to expose him to positive experiences when he's on
his own. The challenge is this: How do you make sure your puppy
stays under threshold? Unlike with people, we can't ask our dogs
how they are feeling, but we can learn to recognize their body
language. When it comes to separation anxiety, body language is
key.

Let's go over a few canine communication pointers.

"He's perfectly fine."

This is how your puppy should be most of the time. His face
and body are loose and relaxed. Whether he's sitting, standing, or
lying, he doesn't carry tension in his body. His eyes are relaxed, and
he might even give you a doggie smile.

"He's holding it together."

Your puppy is beginning to feel uncomfortable. He's alert and
is worried. At this point, he doesn't panic, and he doesn't freak

s holding it together—just. You might start to see slight ...ing, repeated lip licking, furrowed brows, and eyes starting to ...ook bigger, exposing the whites of his eyes. His body will carry more tension, and his face and ears will lose the relaxed look.

"He's freaking out."

Your puppy has lost the ability to control his anxiety and panic. He can no longer hold it together and has gone over his threshold. The more obvious signs are barking, whining, trembling, and shaking. The chewing or destroying routine has started. Any pacing, panting, or lip licking will become exaggerated.

Some puppies don't show their fear so overtly. They may freeze or make themselves small. With these puppies, it's important to take a very close look at their face (eyes, ears, and mouth).

When your puppy panics and passes his tipping point, you will see a full-on meltdown. His fear is taking over, and it can be hard to help calm him down.

We know that humans who suffer from panic attacks often experience vicious cycles of panic. The physical side effects of panic are so unpleasant that the person suffering the attack will panic at feeling panicked. It's possible that dogs experience the same cycle. Hence, they are right to think that you going out is a bad thing, because every time you go out, they feel terrible. The cycle of fear is reinforcing.

It's essential to avoid having your puppy reach his panic mode. We need to break the rigid association between being home alone and fear.

How to Know When Your Puppy Is over Threshold

You need to become an expert at observing body language. Relaxed body language is straightforward, and by now you are likely very good at seeing what your puppy's over-threshold behavior looks like. The tipping point of "holding it together" is harder to spot, and that's where video footage can really help you see and understand the in-between.

If you did the exercise in Chapter 3 in which I asked you to become an expert in your puppy's body language ("Observing Your Puppy" section), you'll find it easier to spot the signs that your puppy is anxious.

By keeping your puppy below his anxiety threshold at all times when home alone, you'll teach him that being alone isn't terrifying. He'll learn to cope on his own, and those panic attacks can become a thing of the past.

What Methods Don't Work for Separation Anxiety (and Why)

There's plenty of pseudo-science in the world of dog training, and none more than when it comes to separation anxiety.

When you tackle separation anxiety you need to focus on the cause of the problem: Your puppy is frightened of being home alone. Lots of advice and plenty of products focus on suppressing the symptoms, but you can't stop the symptoms until you work on the cause. Not only that, but many approaches that aim to do away with the symptoms are often inhumane.

Let's have a look at some examples of products that try to suppress the symptoms of anxiety.

1. Chew Spray

Chew spray seems harmless enough. I mean, it's just an unpleasant taste, right? But it will only stop your puppy from chewing if the taste is sufficiently disgusting to him. It's the equivalent of making someone reduce their calorie intake by putting vomit on their dinner. Sorry for the horrible analogy, but that is exactly what chew spray aims to do. If it does stop your puppy from chewing (big *if*), it doesn't make your puppy feel better about being home.

2. Bark Collars

Bark collars either deliver an electric shock or they spray citronella at close range to your puppy. The aim is to scare your puppy into stopping the home-alone barking. Shock collars use pain and citronella collars work because dogs find citrus smells disgusting. Both are incredibly inhumane, even though the manufacturers don't tell you this. They don't tell you because they don't have to and because you might be horrified to learn that's how they work.

Again, if and when they work, they do so by forcibly suppressing the bark. They don't work on the cause of the barking: your puppy's fear. What about people, though, who say they used the bark collar once and it worked so well that they only have to put the collar on and the puppy won't bark? There's an explanation for this. If the initial shock was sufficiently strong, it would frighten the puppy so much that even just putting the collar on could be enough to intimidate the puppy into stopping. So, yes, there may be no need to shock. Instead the puppy is scared and intimidated by the threat of the shock.

Whichever way these work, it's not pleasant, is it?

3. Indestructible Crates

Indestructible crates, sometimes called anxiety crates, are sold as the only thing you'll need to fix separation anxiety. However, as I explain in the "'Anxiety Crates' Aren't the Answer" section in Chapter 3, most puppies who are fearful of being alone will also hate being confined in a crate. You might stop the damage to your home, but you won't stop their anxiety at being left.

Not only do none of these methods treat separation anxiety, they actually risk making your puppy's separation anxiety worse, as your puppy starts to associate being left alone with a disgusting taste or a painful shock.

If you've tried any of these already, don't feel guilty. Marketers put their spin on them, and it's easy to believe their promises. Instead of feeling guilty, focus on the kind, humane method that does tackle the cause of separation anxiety: gradual exposure.

Gradual Exposure Training Steps Explained

If you've reached this part in the book and still have a puppy who can't be left, then it's time to start desensitizing your puppy to alone time with gradual exposure training, or what I call SubThreshold Training.

Here are the steps:

- Step 1: Assess What your Puppy Can Do Now

- Step 2: Develop a Plan for Your Pre-Departure Cues

- Step 3: Do Your First Gradual Exposure Exercise

- Step 4: Take Good Notes on Your Training

- Step 5: Do Subsequent Exercises

- Step 6: Manage All Absences

Let's go through all of those in detail.

Step 1: Assess What Your Puppy Can Do Now

Often, when we approach any kind of dog training, we focus on where we want our dog to end up. We have a goal in mind, whether that's teaching the dog to sit or to come away from squirrels at the park or to be able to be left on his own for four hours. We might be clear about what we want from training, but so often we miss this question: What can our puppy do now?

We must know where we're starting so we can be clear about the path. So the very first thing we do in separation anxiety training is work out what your puppy can comfortably cope with right now. A common mistake is to guess, or estimate, a starting point. You might say, "Yeah, he's usually fine for five minutes, *I think*" or "He's okay for 30 minutes, *I think*."

Desensitization training is a very precise process. It requires precise information about your puppy's ability to cope on his own. It's not good enough to say you think it might be five minutes or 30 minutes. We need to know, based on observable data.

We get this data by doing a baseline assessment. You are answering "What can your puppy do now?"

When you do this, you need to do some detective work: leave your puppy alone, watch your puppy live on video, and stop the session the moment he starts to seem at all upset.

Use Video for Your Baseline Assessment

Video is a game-changer for treating separation anxiety. It allows us to assess and monitor the puppy's condition in a way that we could never have done in the past. We need to know how he's doing when he's home alone during that training. Without video, how do we do that?

In the past, we might try to sneak a peek through the curtains. With video, we can see in real time exactly how your puppy is doing. This takes away the guesswork.

Set Up a Camera

You have many camera options to use for the assessment and to monitor your puppy when you're out.

First, you can set up video-to-video calls. In that case, you would set up, say, two Zoom accounts, or use your Facebook account and your partner's Facebook account, and set up a video between those two accounts, using smartphones, a laptop, or a tablet. One of the device cameras will focus on your puppy and the other device will be your monitor.

Second, you can turn old smartphones and tablets into cameras. You can find a range of apps for them in the App Store or Play Store. Search for "dogcam app" or "baby monitor app."

Third, you can buy a specific piece of technology, such as a webcam or a surveillance cam. This used to be an expensive approach, but webcams, dogcams, and nannycams have tumbled in price over the years. The great advantage of the third option is you have a device that's set up to go all of the time, so you don't have to worry when you're ready to train.

Carry Out the Baseline Assessment

With a camera in place, you are ready to conduct the baseline assessment. Here are the steps:

1. Go out the door.

2. Stand on the other side of the door with a live video of your puppy on your screen.

3. Monitor your puppy to see how long it takes until he starts to get anxious. Don't let the exercise go for any longer than that. You are looking for the *slightest* signs of anxiety. You only need to determine the amount of time that's passed when he starts to get anxious. You don't need to leave him barking, or whining, or crying, or chewing, or destroying.

Lots of people worry when they do the baseline assessment that they're going to come back to a terrible surprise like their puppy having soiled the carpet or chewed the door.

However, you only step outside for as long as it takes your puppy to start to get the slightest bit anxious, then you come straight back in. You don't leave your puppy long enough to damage or make a mess.

You're looking for that first bark, whine, paw at the door, or whatever your puppy does when he first starts to stress. You want to come back on the "a" of anxious.

When you do the assessment do so without putting on your coat or picking up your purse. Just go straight out. I explain why in the section on pre-departure cues later in this chapter.

Record the Assessment Time

Whatever time you write down is your baseline assessment. Usually the time you record in that baseline assessment is significantly less than you expected. You may have noted seconds, or it may have been minutes, but it probably wasn't as long as you were expecting.

If you can't even get out of the door without your puppy freaking out, skip ahead to the section on the exercise I call "The Door Is a Bore" later in this chapter.

Step 2: Develop a Plan for Your Pre-Departure Cues

Your puppy might have figured out when you're going to leave even before you're near the door. For example, your puppy might have worked out that when you pick up your keys, put on your shoes, and pick up a bag, you're going to leave. These are called pre-departure cues. Your puppy might even pick up on things like brushing teeth or showering. Any part of your routine can be a cue for your puppy that you're about to leave the house.

How Do Dogs Know What These Cues Mean?

Dogs are brilliant at making connections—and puppies are no different. They constantly scan their environment to find tip-offs to what predicts what. They look for associations and connect the dots. Puppies and dogs are prediction-making machines.

A perfect example of a tip-off is a dog bowl. That metal dish with paw prints around the rim doesn't mean anything to your puppy when he first sees it. Puppies aren't born into the world thinking that tin bowls are amazing.

Your puppy starts to associate the bowl with dinner, and dinner is fun. So, when you pick up the bowl, your puppy knows something good is about to happen.

You could try an experiment to show how meaningless your puppies dinner bowl could be. Pick up the bowl repeatedly. Each time you pick up the bowl, you might notice that your puppy gets less and less and less excited.

If you did that a dozen or maybe 20 times in a row, eventually most puppies think, "Oh, okay. I used to think that bowl meant dinner. But she picks it up, and dinner doesn't happen. So now I'm not so sure." You've just started to change the association that bowl equals good stuff. (Note that some puppies will get too amped up if you try this. If this is your puppy, don't try it.)

A pre-departure cue is just like the bowl: The cue itself means nothing to the dog. It's the association that matters. With pre-departure cues, the association is that something terrible is about to happen.

Not all pre-departure cues will trigger your puppy. Don't assume that just because you've read somewhere that putting the radio on, for example, will trigger your puppy that the radio is an unwanted pre-departure cue. Remind yourself that cues don't matter unless they predict something to your puppy.

Cueing Anxiety

The big problem with pre-departure cues is that they can cause puppies who have separation anxiety to get anxious even before you go out the door. If your puppy freaks out as soon as you pick up keys, then you won't be able to do gradual exposure exercises without him getting extremely upset.

For this reason we need to separate our departure cues from

our departure exercises. Otherwise, we can't keep our puppy below threshold.

If this is your puppy, here are some tips for handling pre-departure cues:

- Audit pre-departure cues.

- Prioritize.

- Change the association.

Audit Pre-Departure Cues

First, do an audit. Make a note of what you do as you get ready to leave the house. From this list, highlight anything that makes your puppy upset or anxious, and that your puppy pays attention to—the things your puppy uses as tip-offs to you leaving.

You can find a fillable sample worksheet at www.berightbackthebook.com. List your cues in column one of the worksheet.

Prioritize

Go through your list and ask, "If I were doing a practice departure, which of these pre-departure cues are absolutely unavoidable?"

Let me give you an example. If you live in Canada, it's January, your boots are by the door, and there are three feet of snow outside the door, then your boots are essential.

There's nothing you can do unless you are brave enough to step outside in your socks. List anything like this—anything that's essential to you getting out the door—in column two of the worksheet.

Next ask yourself, "What do I *not* absolutely, desperately have to do?" Maybe you don't have to put on a hat, or perhaps you don't have to pick up a bag—at least not when you do the practice departure. You can, and must, avoid incorporating anxiety-inducing cues for now.

Now separate cues into avoidable and unavoidable.

Leave out the avoidable ones for now. Here's why: The reason your puppy finds, say, you putting on the house alarm scary is because you setting the alarm says, "Scary outcome coming up."

If we can make your puppy think you leaving isn't scary, there's a chance he'll no longer worry about the alarm. Why? The alarm-setting now predicts something that doesn't upset him.

As you work on getting your puppy more comfortable being home alone, you may find that the old cues no longer stress him out (or don't stress him out as much).

This advice is different to advice on pre-departure cues you may have read before. Much of the old thinking fails to take into account the best way to set you and your puppy up for success.

Change the Association

If you have unavoidable cues that panic your puppy, you will need to do work on these. Essentially, you're going to change the association.

Remember the exercise of picking up the bowl earlier in this section, in which we were teaching your puppy that the bowl was no longer a cue to dinner? We were changing the association between bowl and food. We made the bowl meaningless.

We're going to do the same with those unavoidable cues that make your puppy anxious. Puppies aren't born fearing keys. If keys make your puppy anxious it's because they predict you leaving. We want to make keys, and all other *unavoidable* pre-departure cues, meaningless. We need to desensitize your puppy to these just as we would desensitize to absences. We're going to do that by picking up keys, or putting on a jacket or whatever, but without actually going out. This might sound familiar to a lot of the advice you see on the internet about picking up various pre-departure cues randomly throughout the day. But a pre-departure cue might send some puppies over their anxiety threshold.

If picking up keys sends your puppy into a panic, picking up keys repeatedly will not desensitize your puppy. It will actually do the opposite. Your puppy will sensitize (that is, become more afraid).

> If you can do departure training without incorporating cues that upset your puppy, do so.

Instead of acting in an "all or nothing" manner, you need to reduce the intensity of the cue that makes him panic.

So with keys, you might need to break this down into steps such as approaching the drawer where you keep the keys, then repeat. Then open the drawer and repeat. Then touch the keys and so on.

Note that you could also choose to makes keys an avoidable cue by keeping them in your pocket all day.

Let's look at another example. If putting on your winter boots freaks out your puppy you might start by repeatedly walking to the closet where you keep your boots.

Then you might open the closet, and repeat until you bore your puppy. Then you might touch the boots, then pick them up, and so on.

You'll see that your puppy starts to react less to what you're doing as you progress. It's almost as if he is saying, "Oh, when she puts her boots on, she doesn't go out, so boots on doesn't always mean going out."

Your goal is to repeat this cue desensitization process until your puppy stops caring about the triggers.

You want to get to the point where, when you put on your jacket or pick up keys, or whatever, your puppy's reaction is "Oh, that means nothing."

This is true desensitization to pre-departure cues. It might well be different to the outdated and unsafe advice you might have read about departure cues. But this method doesn't risk making your puppy worse.

A crucial point to note is that you only want to desensitize to unavoidable cues.

I cannot stress enough that if you can do departure training without incorporating cues that upset your puppy, do so.

It's worth noting that pre-departure cues can be things that happen after you close the door, not just what happens in the house.

Here's an example of a plan I've used with clients whose dogs are uncomfortable with them driving off.

1. Keep car keys in pocket all day (avoidable cue).

2. Walk toward car.

3. Unlock car.

4. Open and quickly close car door (very gently).

5. Open and quickly close car door (more naturally now).

6. Open car door, leave open for 5 seconds, then close.

7. Open car door, get in, close door,
   sit in car for 10 seconds.

8. Open car door, get in but don't close door, turn
   on engine, leave for 5 seconds, then turn off.

9. Open car door, get in, close door, turn on engine, leave for 5 seconds, then turn off.

10. Open car door, get in, close door, turn on engine, drive 30 feet, and return

11. Open car door, get in, close door, turn on engine, drive 50 feet, and return.

Once you get to 50 feet you can try driving a couple of blocks away. The biggest challenge with this exercise is that you can't look at your puppy live, unless you recruit a passenger. This means you need to be pretty certain he's going to handle each step.

When Cues Might Actually Help

The assumption is that pre-departure cues are bad. As described previously, they are bad because they trigger your puppy into thinking they are going to be left for longer than they can cope with.

However, don't get hung up on the idea that pre-departure cues are automatically bad.

When people embark on separation anxiety training, I often hear them say, "I'm worried that the camera will become a pre-departure cue." That's reasonable since every time you train you set up a camera. Your puppy starts to notice the camera. That's a problem, isn't it?

Not necessarily.

If you only used the camera during training, when all your absences are safe and below threshold, and if you've never used a camera in the past (when your puppy may have been left longer than he was able to cope with), then setting up your camera will actually signal "Don't worry. This is fine." to your puppy.

The camera has only ever been used when things are going to be okay for the dog. Yes, he might notice it. Yes, he might know it means you're going out. But that doesn't make it a problem.

In fact, there's evidence that whether a cue predicts something good or bad, it might actually help the dog cope. A study carried out in 2020 by the University of Barcelona suggested that dogs coped better with a stressful absence when they could predict it was about to happen. This is in line with the wider body of research into stress theory that it's better to know when something bad is coming than to anticipate it but not be exactly sure when. A 2016 study conducted by researchers at University College, London, in which participants were given a mild electric shock when they lost a life while playing a computer game, showed that uncertainty caused more stress than the inevitable pain.

Ignore the blanket advice that pre-departure cues are bad. We only need to worry about them if the dog associates that cue with something bad about to happen. Even then it might be better to warn the dog that this absence is going to be bad.

Like much to do with separation anxiety training, much depends on context.

Give it a Try

The key takeaway is to work on cues as you need to. The worksheet you filled out previously will help you collect and sort all of the pre-departure cues.

When you first work on departure exercises where you get out of the door, pare down your leaving routine and leave out as many cues as you can. Desensitize your puppy to the unavoidable ones. Then, when you achieve some nice duration—about 15 minutes is ideal—add back in the avoidable cues you previously dropped, one or two at a time. Or get creative and change your leaving routine for the longer term. If putting on your yoga pants somehow cued your puppy that he was going to be okay and meant you could leave him comfortably for two hours, you'd invest in a bunch of new yoga pants, wouldn't you?

Step 3: Do Your First Gradual Exposure Exercise

Once you've done your baseline assessment and have that initial duration, you can begin to do your gradual exposure exercises.

These exercises form the basis for desensitization. You're going to get your puppy used to being alone by showing him alone time is safe, by going slowly, and by doing graduated departures that are short enough that he doesn't get upset.

You will need a training plan for this. Here's how to write one.

Go back to your baseline assessment. The time duration from your assessment is the basis for your first exercise.

When you do a departure, you go out the door for a period of time and come back. Each time you do an exercise you will be coming and going several times. I call those *steps.* So, you have an exercise for the day consisting of a number of steps. For any given step in an exercise, you need to state how long you'll be out the door.

You will have an overall target duration. This will be the last step in the exercise. In addition, you will have shorter durations for the other steps. The target duration you choose for your first exercise should be shorter than the actual duration from your baseline assessment.

Have a look at some examples:

Assessment Time	Target Duration for First Exercise
30 seconds	20 seconds
60 seconds	40 seconds
5 minutes	4 minutes

You have your target duration, but as I noted, each exercise has a number of steps. All of those steps need to be shorter than your target duration. If your target duration is 45 seconds, you just do that as your last step. All the other steps are shorter.

Here's an example using 45 seconds as the target duration:

STEP 1	5 seconds
STEP 2	10 seconds
STEP 3	5 seconds
STEP 4	15 seconds
STEP 5	10 seconds
STEP 6	2 seconds
STEP 7	5 seconds
STEP 8	10 seconds
STEP 9	5 seconds
STEP 10	45 seconds

Notice that I put the target duration at the end of the exercise and that I mixed up the durations. Some were shorter than the previous step. Some were longer.

Remember that these are examples, not the times you should use for your puppy. You need to develop exercises for your puppy based on what he can currently do. (If you want guidance, refer to the sample plans in Appendix A.)

You might be wondering why we have so many different duration steps. Why don't we just go out for 45 seconds, eight times?

With separation anxiety, you going out the door without fuss and without reaction is massive. Yes, duration is important (and that's the goal we tend to get more caught up on), but getting out the door calmly and without fuss is a big part of training.

Each exercise is an opportunity to do both: get out the door and extend duration. The reason I put so many of the shorter steps in each exercise is that there's a high probability your puppy will be able to do these short steps.

So even if your puppy struggles at the new target duration, he still gets lots of solid practice in. And remember what I said earlier about repetition being so important to changing a dog's emotion. We need your puppy to experience lots of the new association of leaving being fine in order to balance out his history of finding absences scary. Even if your puppy has never been left, his separation anxiety means he has a strong negative association of being left and we need plenty of positive association to outweigh the negative.

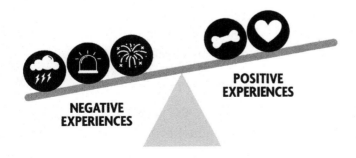

NEGATIVE EXPERIENCES

POSITIVE EXPERIENCES

These shorter steps also act as warm-ups to the longer duration, and lots of dogs do better with a warm-up, especially in the early stages of training.

Note that some dogs do really well with these short, warm-up steps. Others struggle. Using warm-ups is a very dog-dependent decision, so observe your puppy and drop the warm-ups if that works better for your puppy.

Stepping out the Door

Now that you've written your first plan, carry out the exercise. An ideal time to train is when all the SAFE conditions have been met (see Chapter 1 "What's Normal Puppy Behavior and What's Separation Anxiety?" for an explanation of SAFE).

When you're ready to go, set up your video, just as you did for the baseline assessment. You need to be able to see that video of your puppy when you're standing on the other side of the door.

Recording is ideal, because it can be helpful to go back and look at what you've done. It's not essential, but it can make training more effective. If you're struggling to record or your app doesn't record, look into free apps that will record your screen.

Keep your plan handy. Go out the door for however long it says in step one and then come right back in. Step two, same thing.

All the time, look for signs of anxiety and agitation. That's important. If you see your puppy getting stressed when you're on the other side of the door, come back in immediately.

How Long between Each Training Step?

As a general rule of thumb, aim for about 30 to 60 seconds. You don't have to wait a long time between the steps, but vary it. Maybe between steps one and two you do 45 seconds. Between steps two and three you do 30 seconds. Between steps three and four you might do 50 seconds. And so on.

You may find that your puppy is getting more agitated each time you do a step. For example, he's okay during step one, but during step two and then step three he seems more agitated. If this happens, increase the time between steps and see if that helps. Instead of less than a minute between steps try two to three.

You could come back in, hang out on the sofa, check your email, or whatever, but if you find that he needs more time between steps, take that time. If you give the puppy more time between steps and that still doesn't help him calm down, call it a day and repeat the exercise the following day.

When you're on the other side of the door watching your puppy, you need to be absolutely on top of looking for anxiety. No matter how far into the exercise you are or whatever the duration is, when you see anxiety, you need to come back in. That's very, very important.

What Should I Do between the Steps?

Some puppies get more agitated with coming and going. They do worse if you go back in and sit down. Others do worse if you don't sit down. Test this out for your puppy. Maybe you need to hang by the door, and just go in and out. Maybe you need to come back and just wander around doing a simple chore or two. Find out what works for your puppy.

What if He's Barking?

We've all been told that we shouldn't reinforce barking by coming back in when a dog howls. And yes, this is definitely something that we try to discourage in non-anxious puppies. If your non-anxious puppy is barking for something, try not to reward the puppy by giving him what he wants. If your puppy who has separation anxiety is barking for you to come back, should you ignore until he stops?

Well, no. As we explored earlier, if you leave a puppy who has separation anxiety to bark, he's only going to get more anxious. Coming back in while your puppy is barking isn't ideal—but the downside is that, if you don't come back, you're making the anxiety worse.

You must make a choice. The best choice is to come back in, because you don't want anxiety to worsen. That's way harder to deal with than a puppy you just reinforced for barking when you came back in.

The best solution of all is to keep absences short enough that your puppy doesn't bark to begin with.

How Is Your Puppy When You Come Back?

Excessive greeting used to be seen as a sign of separation anxiety, but we now know it's actually not something exclusive to dogs who have separation anxiety.

Lots of puppies and adult dogs greet excitedly when you come back through the door. Lots of dogs greet strangers who come to visit excitedly. An excited greeting on its own doesn't mean that your puppy is either upset or stressed or anxious. He might just be really pleased to see you.

What's excessive for one puppy might be nothing out of the ordinary for another. The first thing I ask clients when they tell me about their over-the-top greeter is "What's the norm for your puppy?"

Determining a Normal Greeting

We need to establish how your puppy normally greets. Then we can assess whether the greeting after being left alone is excessive and potentially a sign of stress. Here's how to do so:

1. Note what he does when you come back after some time alone. What does he do: bark, jump up, pant? How long does he take to calm down?

2. Consider how he would be had he stayed home with someone else in the house (could be family, could be a sitter). When you return, does he act:

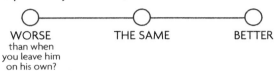

WORSE
than when
you leave him
on his own?   THE SAME   BETTER

3. Now consider how he reacts when he goes out (with a dog walker or family). How is his greeting when he comes home? Use the same scale as with #2. Does he react:

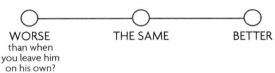

WORSE
than when
you leave him
on his own?   THE SAME   BETTER

4. Think about what he's like when people he knows (not people in your household, but friends or other family members) come to the house. Again, using the same scale, when they step in the door, does he react:

WORSE
than when
you leave him
on his own?   THE SAME   BETTER

If he always greets more excessively in scenario #1, there's a good chance it's caused by the stress of being home alone. In this case, the best way to tackle the greeting is by working on his anxiety.

If your puppy isn't stressed on his own and is just a super-excitable type, then you can try other tactics. These might include:

- Teaching him a rock-solid sit or down. He can't jump while he's doing one of these!

- Doing some simple training such as hand touches or "puppy push-ups" (sit-down-sit-down). These are great for puppies who are too bouncy to hold a sit- or down-stay when excited.

- Giving him a task, like finding a toy, or picking up your shoes and helping you put them away.

We used to think that ignoring a puppy was the best way to calm him down. But ignoring a dog who doesn't just want your attention but *needs* your attention is quite punishing.

And if you've ever tried to do that, you know:

- How tough this can be when your puppy acts giddy,

- That ignoring him doesn't seem to make much difference, and

- That it's hard on you too when you only want to ruffle his ears after not seeing him all day!

Getting him to do something else is much more effective—and way more fun for both of you.

Step 4: Take Good Notes on Your Training

When you've done the final step of your exercise, record data about the session. (You can find a sample worksheet at www.berightbackthebook.com.)

Record things like what he ate that day, how much exercise he had, who did the departure, and who was around. (You'll see more examples in the sample worksheet.)

Make sure you capture data every single time, even if it doesn't seem like it makes much sense at the time. Over time, trends may emerge. For example, maybe he does better at 2:00 p.m., maybe he does better after he's eaten his dinner, maybe he does better before his dinner, and so on.

Our natural tendency as human beings is to want to see progress. Every time we do one of these exercises, we want to see that he did better than yesterday, and that tomorrow is better than today. But the thing is, progress with training is never a straight line.

If you've ever had to learn anything complicated, you know it usually isn't a gradual or linear procession day after day after day. Also remember we're trying to change your puppy's emotion, not just teach him a new trick. Don't be worried if you don't have a string of good days. Bad days will happen (and we talk about how to deal with that later in the book).

Step 5: Do Subsequent Exercises

The first exercise was built around your target duration, with a number of steps around that. You'll do the same for exercise #2. But how do you decide what this target duration should be?

If your dog did well with exercise #1, make the duration a bit longer. Make it a bit harder for him—but not too, too hard. You don't want to double the time, for example.

Construct another exercise that has several short steps—times that are shorter than the target duration—followed by the target duration as the last step.

Every time he does well with an exercise, increase the duration the next time you train. As your duration increases, you reduce the total number of steps so that the overall time you are training is reasonable.

If you have a day when he doesn't meet target duration, you have a couple options:

1. If your dog was close to the target duration, try the same exercise again the following day, or

2. If he was way off, give him an easier one the following day.

I much prefer option #2, as it puts less pressure on your puppy and you.

With separation anxiety training, we go slow to go fast. If we push too quickly, as is our tendency, we make the process slower overall because we're not respecting the puppy's pace. We're not understanding what his threshold is and what he's comfortable with.

Never worry about dropping back in duration. If you do drop back, chances are you'll have a successful exercise, and that's what's important. Try not to get too hung up on constantly pushing for longer durations.

How Often Should I Train?

In terms of frequency, do the training four or five times a week. You don't have to do it every day, and you want to take days off. Just like humans' brains do, dogs' brains get tired. A rest day can really help you and him.

How Long Should Training Take?

This is among the most important questions for most owners. And who can blame you? Your life is on hold.

Separation anxiety training is different from most training you might have done. If you've taught your puppy to sit, to come when called, or to walk on a loose leash, you know that you can make some progress quite quickly with all of those things. With a good plan, lots of great treats, and the right guidance, you can train a puppy to sit in an hour, if not in minutes. But separation anxiety isn't teaching a new obedience behavior. Changing a puppy's emotion is fundamentally different from obedience training.

A better way to think of it is grief counseling or divorce counseling. When people go through severe emotional trauma, everyone takes their own time. No two people are alike in the time to recovery.

> ❚❚ Separation anxiety is most definitely an emotional trauma.

If somebody went through a difficult divorce, would you ask, "How long does it take to get over a divorce?" You may, but you're not going to get a concrete answer. It depends on the person. It depends on their situation and what led to divorce. It depends also on what they've done in terms of talk therapy or any other things they've done to help themselves through.

Predicting how long it will take any being, whether a human or a dog, to get over an emotional trauma is difficult. Separation anxiety is most definitely an emotional trauma.

Six to 12 months would be a reasonable estimate. Some puppies get through it in three months, and some puppies can take longer than a year. It is impossible to precisely predict.

Even though we can't predict how long your puppy will take to get over separation anxiety, we can control some things that make it go either more quickly or slower.

Rather than think, "How long is recovery going to take?" think, "How can I make recovery go as well as it possibly could?"

Here are some ways that can make it go more quickly:

1. Train regularly.

2. Don't train too often (or too infrequently). The sweet spot is about five times a week.

3. Train with a plan.

4. Use a video to monitor your puppy's anxiety.

5. Never let your puppy go over threshold while you train (or at any other time).

6. Don't push too hard with your exercises. Don't get greedy about duration. Drop back if your puppy is struggling and only push ahead if he's doing well.

7. Don't leave your puppy alone for longer than he can handle.

You can also do some things that can make the training go worse/slower:

1. Leave your puppy for way longer than he can cope. The problem with that is you're trying to send the message to your puppy that being alone isn't scary. During the training, you have nice, safe absences. Leaving him for longer than he can cope undoes the message that being on your own is safe and therefore slows our effort.

2. Train too much (or too little).

3. Get greedy and push too much.

4. Be unorganized. Don't have a plan.

5. Train without watching your puppy on video.

Step 6: Manage All Absences

Because going over threshold can be such a deal-breaker to training, I can't stress enough the importance of finding a way not to leave your dog.

This sounds ridiculous: If your puppy could be looked after 24/7, you wouldn't worry about separation anxiety. But remember: You must send the message to the puppy that being on his own is safe, so you can't have any scary absences while you're training.

What if you can't find a way to not leave, nor to get somebody to look after your puppy 24/7 tomorrow? Does that mean you shouldn't start training? There's a good chance your puppy isn't going to get over separation anxiety while he's also being left, though a small number of puppies do seem to make progress despite being left.

You definitely can't leave him as much as you're leaving him today, but if you can't make sure he has company 100% of the time, why not see, next week, if you can leave him for one day less or one hour less, and then start the training? Then the week after, leave him for a bit less, and even less, and so on.

When people change habits, some can do it cold turkey, and some need more of a gradual change. If you're the latter, try it. Making one change to your schedule next week means he's left a little bit less often than he is now.

Ultimately, people quickly realize they need to stop leaving their dog because they just don't see the progress in training. On top of that, if your puppy is barking or chewing or soiling in the house, the only way to stop that problem behavior is to stop the absences. Managing not only helps training go better, it stops the immediate problem, too.

It was notable to see how many people who, when the pandemic started and they were able to reduce the amount of time their anxious dog was left alone, remarked that their dog had seemed less anxious overall just by them no longer leaving their dog.

If all else fails and you have no option but to leave your puppy, start your training while you're looking for a way to stop leaving him. Remember that if you have to leave him, he's not in a good place, he's over his threshold, and he's in a blind panic when you go out. From a humane perspective, if you could relieve even some of that panic, that would be such a win for you and your puppy.

I've been accused of being unrealistic when I talk about managing absences. Some reviewers of my last book said that my method only works for people in a certain income bracket. This just isn't the case. I've seen people from all walks of life and from very different financial situations make this work.

It's never easy. But it can be done.

What if You Have an Emergency?

If you are managing absences but an emergency comes up, say, your puppy is likely going to have a bad time because you are leaving him for longer than he can handle. However, there are steps you can take to mitigate this.

The following summarizes what you can do before leaving for an unavoidable emergency scary departure and during training:

TYPE OF ABSENCE	CUES
A safe training absence	Use a brand-new cue to signify "I'm going out, but this is going to be fine." It will be meaningless to your puppy at first, but he'll soon connect the dots. The cues you might use: • *Something physical, like picking up a large book before you leave* • *A verbal cue (A favorite of mine, that a client used, was "shenanigans.")* • *A hand signal such as both thumbs up*
An unavoidable over-threshold absence	Don't use any of your new cues. Make your leaving routine more similar to the past.

Note: I urge you not to train for the "unavoidable over-threshold absence." This is an emergency situation.

The Door Is a Bore! Desensitizing to the Door

Desensitizing to the door is a wonderful exercise for all puppies, not just those whose threshold is so low you cannot step out the door.

I often liken separation anxiety training to gradual exposure therapy for people with a fear of flying. As much as we try with desensitization to make the steps as small and gradual as we can, there comes a point with both separation anxiety and fear of flying where there is a cliff edge. With separation anxiety it's stepping out and closing the door. With flying it's takeoff.

Both are monumental for the subject.

However, we can do our best to make stepping out gradual and incremental. (The same can't be said of a plane taking off, of course. The aircraft either leaves the runway or it doesn't!) Luckily we can work on the issue of the door in small enough steps that work for nearly all puppies.

Break down your approach into small, independent steps. An example Door Is a Bore plan might look like this:

1. Walk to within 6 feet of door.

2. Walk to within 3 feet of door.

3. Walk to door and touch door.

4. Walk to door and touch door handle.

5. Walk to door and depress door handle.

6. Walk to door and touch lock.

7. Walk to door and turn lock.

8. Walk to door, open door, close door.

9. Walk to door, open door for three seconds, close door.

10. Walk to door, open door, step through door without closing.

11. Walk to door, open door, step through door, close door, open door, step back inside.

12. Walk to door, open door, step through door, close door, count to 2, open door, step back inside.

13. Walk to door, open door, step through door, close door, count to 3, open door, step back inside.

14. Walk to door, open door, step through door, close door, count to 4, open door, step back inside.

15. Walk to door, open door, step through door, close door, count to 5, open door, step back inside.

Doors are exciting for puppies. We want to teach puppies that, just because the door opens, doesn't mean anything bad or exciting is going to happen. Hence, I call this exercise "Door Is a Bore." We want your puppy to think, "Oh, the door opening? So dull."

You can practice Door Is a Bore training several times a day. It's great for days when you don't have much time. It's wonderful for building confidence after a training blip or a break, and it's even helpful as a warm-up to actual departures. I encourage you to use it regularly. Spending time on Door Is a Bore is always time well-spent.

Now, if your puppy gets amped up as you go to and from the door, omit the walking to the door element. Just start by the door, as follows:

1. Walk to door and just hang out there for a couple of minutes.

2. Touch door handle.

3. Depress door handle.

4. Touch lock.

5. Turn lock.

6. Open door, close door.

7. Open door for three seconds, close door.

8. Open door, step through door without closing.

9. Open door, step through door, close door, open door, step back inside.

10. Open door, step through door, close door, open door, step back inside.

If your puppy still gets excited, try plan outlined in "The Magic Mat Game" section in this chapter.

Once your puppy is acing the Door is a Bore training you can progress to the departure training outlined in "Gradual Exposure Training Steps Explained" earlier this chapter.

Desensitizing to You Getting Up

Since you getting up off the sofa can be a huge trigger to a puppy who's worried about you leaving, you can use the same principles used in door desensitization to get your puppy to not react when you get up.

Your plan might look something like this:

- Start to get up but only get about 1 foot out of your seat.

- Stand up.

- Stand up and take two steps.

- Stand up and take three steps.

You might keep adding steps until you can walk across the room, for example.

Is it a Problem if Your Puppy Follows You?

Following is one of the most confusing presenting behaviors in separation anxiety. Following used to been seen as an indicator that the puppy was anxious about the owner leaving. However, this is another one of those puppy separation anxiety myths, since following an owner around is a natural behavior for dogs, especially puppies. Anxious and non-anxious puppies like to follow.

You are the source of all things fun and exciting. Puppies are curious and learning. No wonder, then, that they decide to follow you around the house.

Now, it's true that some puppies follow more than others. And some puppies follow everywhere, all the time. The latter can be frustrating. If this is your puppy, you've probably reached the stage where you just want to be able to take a shower in peace or take out the rubbish without a full-on meltdown.

Let's take a look at when you should worry about following and, if your puppy following you is driving you to distraction, what you can do about it.

When You Should Worry about Following

We need to worry about following when the behavior is accompanied by body language that is fearful or anxious.

Remember that when we help puppies to be happy home alone, we are looking for an absence of fear or anxiety. We are not changing behavior with our training method. We are changing how the puppy *feels* about being left. We are behavior-agnostic:

> ❚❚ Our goal is to teach the puppy to feel safe, not to teach the puppy what to do.

We don't care what the puppy does while we're gone as long as the puppy is happy and safe. Obviously we care about puppies getting into electrical cables, or chewing the corner of our expensive new rug, but we don't care whether they stay on their bed, have a good sniff, and wander or sit and look out of the glass doors to the garden.

We just want them to feel safe. We're looking for the absence of fear and anxiety.

This sort of training is very different from most of the other training that we do with puppies. We spend considerable time teaching behaviors (sit, stay, come when called, walk nicely on leash), but we spend less time changing how a puppy feels.

That's why it can be hard to apply desensitization training to puppies. Our goal is to teach the puppy to feel safe, not to teach the puppy what to do. It's natural, then, to focus on a behavior like following, because as owners we're trained to train behavior.

However, with home-alone training, instead of assessing whether the puppy is learning to do something, your focus is assessing whether you can see signs of fear or anxiety.

Doors are super exciting to puppies, as doors mean exciting things: people coming in, or the puppy going out for a walk. No wonder, then, that when you go to the door, your puppy decides to follow. He may do so at a rapid pace. He may do so with some excited whining.

When we're doing separation anxiety training, we don't care as long as there is no fear. The puppy can feel what they want as long as there's no fear.

A word about the puppy being relaxed: You might often hear

people say that in order for home-alone training to be effective, the puppy needs to be relaxed. Relaxed isn't the opposite of scared, though.

Think about it: A puppy could be excited, curious, playful, confused, baffled, and amped-up, and not be scared. None of these are relaxed behaviors, and none are signs that the puppy is scared. Instead of "Is the puppy relaxed?" I prefer the distinction "scared/not scared." If we use that categorization then whatever the puppy does when we leave is fine.

Hence, using following as an indicator of home-alone training success gives us a false read and will stop us from progressing. We need to worry about following when the behavior is accompanied by body language that is fearful or anxious. In the absence of that body language, we can let the puppy follow.

When Teaching a Puppy Not to Follow Is Worth It

In some cases working on home-alone training is all you need to do to resolve following. I've definitely seen case after case in which, once the dog is comfortable with being left, they shadow less. It's almost as if they can now stop worrying about where their owners are, or they no longer think their owner is about to head out and leave them to deal with a scary absence.

However, there are times when your puppy following you around the house just gets to be too much. If you can't cope with your puppy wanting to go everywhere you go, here's what you can do about it:

1. Double down on crate training, knowing that even anxious puppies can eventually learn to be okay.

2. Teach your puppy to stay on a mat while you move around the house using the Magic Mat training routine.
   Note you don't need to do both #1 and #2. Instead, pick one.

You will get lots of advice to work on your puppy not following you around the home as a means to help your puppy overcome separation anxiety, whether this training is referred to as the "no follow" routine, independence training, or boundary work.

As I hope I have impressed on you throughout this book, my approach to training is all about efficiency. As a dog owner, you have limited time, energy, and patience. Focus your effort on the training that is most likely to result in your dog being comfortable at home alone. That's *gradual exposure to home-alone time*.

Dealing with Door Dashers

One challenge you might encounter with your enthusiastic puppy who charges to the door when you approach is them dashing out of the house.

We know that doors are exciting to puppies. For some puppies, opening the door is so exciting that they attempt to rush past you as soon as you open it.

If your puppy does this, then you'll need to take some precautionary steps when you do home-alone training:

- **Use a baby gate in the hallway or doorway so that your puppy can't get to the door.** He may try to dash through the baby gate as you open it, but your puppy won't be running into the street. I normally recommend not using a baby gate when doing alone-time training because, for many puppies, it just creates an extra sense of isolation. However, for door dashers, safety must come first. If your puppy really struggles with the extra barrier, use a freestanding gate or exercise pen and put it *outside* your door. That will catch him if he does exit.

- **Teach your puppy to stay when you step out.** You can use the Magic Mat training plan for this. Your puppy doesn't have to hold the stay for the whole time you're out. Your goal is just to get him to hold the stay long enough that you can exit without him sneaking out. The Magic Mat teaches a down stay as the foundational behavior, but you could use a sit stay if you prefer.

- **The simplest and most obvious solution is just to gently hold your puppy back as you leave, stepping around him to get out of the door.** Be careful not to be rough with him. It's easy to exert force with a puppy who's trying to run out. Your goal is to prevent him from dashing, not scare him.

This last option might not work with a puppy who's quick or one who is so tiny it's hard to get down to him in time.

The Magic Mat Game

The Magic Mat Game will teach your puppy that it's way more rewarding to stay on his mat than to do other behaviors.

You can use the Magic Mat for puppies who:

- Are hyper-attached (see "Tips for Hyper-Attached Puppies" in this chapter for a definition of hyper-attachment).

- Bark at outside noises and need to learn an alternative behavior (see "Watchdog or Alarm Barking" in Chapter 6).

- Struggle to sleep on their own (see "Nighttime Anxiety" in Chapter 6)

- Dash out the door (see "Dealing with Door Dashers" earlier in this chapter).

- Get over-excited by repeated steps in departure training (see "Gradual Exposure Training Steps Explained" previously in this chapter).

You will need:

- A mat that you'll only use for this training (and will put away when not training),

- Lots of great treats

- The training plan outlined later in this section, and

- The demo video (see www.berightbackthebook.com).

"Grading" Rules:

- Work in sets of five tries.

- If your puppy gets it right four or five times out of five, move to the next step.

- If your puppy gets it right three times out of five, repeat the current step.

- If your puppy gets it right one or two times out of five, drop to the previous step.

- Always reward your puppy in a down position. If he gets up when you're reaching for treats he just earned, get him back into a down before giving him the treat.

The more you practice this, the more magic the mat will become. When you take out the mat, your puppy will rush to it. This is because all that reward training you've been doing has made him associate the mat with treats!

Once this behavior is solid, you can start to take the mat on the road, which is great for trips to the vets, visiting friends, or even eating out (in places where that's allowed).

Here's the plan:

STEP #	WHAT YOUR PUPPY NEEDS TO DO TO EARN TREATS
1.	Hold a down for 1 second with a treat ~2 feet away from the dog at his nose level.
2.	Hold a down for 3 seconds with a treat ~2 feet away from the dog at his nose level.
3.	Hold a down for 1 second with a treat 2–3 feet away on the ground. (If he moves, cover or grab the treat so he can't pick it up.)
4.	Hold a down for 3 seconds with a treat 2–3 feet away on the ground.
5.	(Stand on the other side of your puppy.) Hold a down for 1 second with a treat 2–3 feet away on the ground.
6.	(Stand on the other side of your puppy.) Hold a down for 3 seconds with a treat 2–3 feet away on the ground.
7.	Hold a down while you take 1 step to the side and back.
8.	Hold a down while you take 2 steps to the side and back.
9.	Hold a down while you take 3 steps around your puppy and back.
10.	Hold a down while you walk halfway around your puppy and back.
11.	Hold a down while you walk a full circle around your puppy.
12.	Repeat steps 7–11 in the other direction.
13.	Hold a down while you walk 6 feet across the room and return immediately.
14.	Hold a down while you step to doorway and return immediately.
15.	Hold a down while you step out of the room into hallway and return immediately.

STEP #	WHAT YOUR PUPPY NEEDS TO DO TO EARN TREATS
16.	Hold a down while you step out of the room, close door, and return immediately.
17.	Hold a down while you go into an adjoining room and return immediately.
18.	Hold a down while you go into an adjoining room, close door, and return immediately.
19.	Hold a down while you step to doorway and return immediately.
20.	Hold a down while you step out of the room into the hallway and return immediately.
21.	Hold a down while you step out of the room into the hallway, into another room, and return immediately.
22.	Hold a down while you step out of the room into the hallway, into another room, count to 10, then return.
23.	Hold a down while you step out of the room into the hallway, into another room, count to 20, then return.

From here, continue to build duration in another room. If you have stairs, you could add in going up stairs. You might want to break it down into a few steps at a time.

What if your puppy can't go into a down on cue yet? Check out the plan to teach your puppy at www.berightbackthebook.com.

Tips for Hyper-Attached Puppies

When a puppy gets anxious if they aren't by their owner's side, it can be near impossible to keep them below threshold and anxiety-free. This can hinder training. It's also extremely stressful for the owner who knows that—no matter what they do to find care for their puppy—chances are, their puppy is having a bad time.

If this is your puppy, here are my two top tips for coping with a puppy who can't leave your side.

1. Spread the Love

This idea comes from the world of child psychology. When a child is overly attached to one parent, getting the non-favored parent more involved in fun activities and reducing the favored-parent involvement can help.

With separation anxiety, I advise getting at least two to three other people to do more of the fun stuff in the puppy's life, while the current main caregiver reduces their involvement. The goal is for the dog to see both that they don't need to rely on just one person for good things to happen and that they can be safe with others.

The other people don't have to be family members. They might be the dog sitter, daycare staff, or a friend. Make sure that these are people who can commit to being a pretty permanent part of the dog's life.

Try not to throw your puppy in at the deep end when you get others involved. By that I mean if your puppy panics without you, start by leaving him with new people for only a short period of time—a few minutes ideally.

When you do leave him with someone else, they should hand-feed him his favorite treats and play his favorite games.

If he won't take treats it's likely that the absence from you was too much for him. Just go back to spreading the love for a week or so, then try again.

2. Find the "Least Worst" Alternative to You

Once you are able to leave your puppy with someone else because you've being doing all that good work in spreading the love, you're going to find he's happier with some people than with others.

Here you would rank different care scenarios from scariest to best. *Scariest* would be being on their own. *Best* would be being with their special person.

Maybe your dog gets stressed when left with the dog sitter—but not as stressed as they are at daycare. Or maybe they are okay with your partner—but better than when they are with your parents.

Find a scenario that is the "least worst," and choose that as your first option for care. You can tie this in with tip #1 to get your dog to be comfortable with someone other than you.

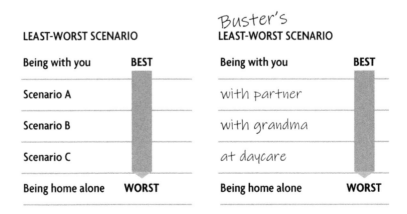

LEAST-WORST SCENARIO		*Buster's* LEAST-WORST SCENARIO	
Being with you	**BEST**	Being with you	**BEST**
Scenario A		*with partner*	
Scenario B		*with grandma*	
Scenario C		*at daycare*	
Being home alone	**WORST**	Being home alone	**WORST**

Remember you didn't give birth to your puppy. He just chose to attach himself to you. And if he can attach himself to you, he can develop attachments to others too.

Training Considerations

Separation anxiety training probably seems very different from other training that you practice with your puppy. You might be teaching him to sit, to come when called, to sit when visitors arrive, to walk nicely on leash. All of these require your puppy to do something. The behavior he performs matters. When you ask your puppy to perform a new behavior you're most likely using food or games to reward your puppy when he gets it right.

When we change a dog's emotion, however, we care less about what he does than how he feels.

Our goal is to make him feel better about being home alone. When we stop him feeling scared about being left, we will also stop the behavior that's caused by his fear—behavior such as barking, destroying, soiling, and so on.

The different approach that we take with separation anxiety means that we need to adopt a new perspective on a number of factors. Let's have a look at those.

Relaxed Isn't Always the Opposite of Anxious

We assume that if a dog doesn't feel anxious, he will "relax," by which we typically mean lie down. We expect to see him lying on his bed or snoozing on the sofa. But think about it: If you're not feeling anxious, are you relaxing? Maybe. Maybe not. You might be out for a run, or watching an exciting sports match, or singing your heart out to the radio while dancing around the house.

No anxiety, but definitely not lying down anywhere. It's the same for dogs. They can be relaxed without doing the things that

▟▟ When we do separation anxiety training exercises, we're doing something pretty unnatural: We're going out of the door and coming back, over and over. Who does that?

we stereotype as being relaxation.

All we're looking for is for him not to be anxious.

This means your puppy can walk around the house, look out of the window, or even sit and look at the door if he wants. As long as he's not stressed out, he can do whatever he wants.

It's Okay if Your Puppy Plays the Waiting Game

When we do separation anxiety training exercises, we're doing something pretty unnatural: We're going out of the door and coming back, over and over. Who does that?

Not only is it weird to us, it's weird to our dogs. As a result, it's perfectly natural for them to watch us and follow us, no doubt wondering what we're doing.

When we work on short durations, they get used to us coming back quickly. It makes sense for them to hang out by the door, especially since they know we're coming back.

This door waiting used to be a cause for concern. You'd hear trainers say that fixating on the door must mean that the dog is anxious. However, in the context of a separation anxiety exercise, it's reasonable behavior. Doors are exciting to dogs. You're coming and going. He's curious as to what you're doing. No wonder he waits.

As you build up duration, you might expect the waiting to stop. But it doesn't always. Here's why: Have you ever waited for a bus that was late? You know they should run every five minutes, but you've been waiting for 10. Therefore, you give up and decide to walk instead.

Only you don't. Instead you say, "I've been waiting so long it must come any minute now." And you repeat that as you stand at the chilly bus stop: "Any minute now."

You see, you've been conditioned to expect that the bus runs regularly, so the longer you wait, the more convinced you are that it must be coming "any minute now."

With the dog who waits at the door, it's the same: Your dog gets used to you going out for short bursts and returning in seconds. If we could go inside his head, we might hear him say, "Any second now." As you increase your time, his expectation doesn't decrease. In fact, he's more likely to assume you will come back any second.

This is why many dogs, especially during the early stages of training, wait by the door. They aren't anxious, but they are wondering what you're up to.

As I said earlier, we don't care about behavior. Rather, we care about the absence of anxiety. If your puppy decides he wants to wait by the door, then as long as he's not anxious, let him do so.

No Food in Training

Rewards-based training is the best. Dogs love it because it's fun and it doesn't involve fear or pain. Best of all, it works. In fact, research shows that it works better than any other method. Hands down, the best tool for dog training is food. Despite the fabulousness of food, though, it's best left in the cupboard when you're training a dog who has separation anxiety.

It's not that we couldn't use food for separation anxiety training, it's just that we don't need to.

If food is so marvelous why, then, don't we use it for separation anxiety training?

First, separation anxiety training is not about obedience training. Sure, we could try to address separation anxiety by training a reliable down-stay that stops the dog scratching at the door, but even competitive obedience dogs won't hold a stay the whole time you're at work.

Second, a good number of dogs won't eat while their owner is absent. Interestingly, this includes both dogs who have separation anxiety and non-anxious dogs. Anxious dogs who do eat while you're out tend to chomp, devour, or practically inhale their food. They aren't exactly showing relaxed home-alone behavior.

Third, for those dogs who will eat when you're out, food often just distracts them from the fact you're gone. Once they finish the food, the panic sets in—and a frozen Kong will only last so long.

However, don't drop food entirely from the equation. Food is ideal for use in puzzles to keep busy minds occupied, and this type of enrichment is an important part of the overall treatment program for a dog who has separation anxiety.

Food can also be used as management. For example, if your puppy will eat when you're out and is okay for the time it takes to eat his frozen Kong, use that time to get groceries or pick up the kids from school.

You might have considered using a remote-controlled treat feeder. These aren't cheap, and using them requires a very specific training technique. These can be fine for some dogs, but they don't always help when we're doing separation anxiety training. Here's why:

1. Some dogs stress when the treat shoots out.

2. The treats eventually run out, and then very often your dog freaks out.

3. You have to be watching, so this isn't a solution that always makes sense (when you're going to the movies or driving, for example).

As your puppy becomes increasingly settled with alone time, you can definitely think about adding food puzzles and safe chews back into the mix. Don't rush to do this, though. Adding food back in unsettles lots of puppies.

Family-Friendly Approaches to Training

More than just you in your household? You'll need to take into account how and whether you'll get other people involved with training. Let's take a look at some considerations.

Involving Kids

For those of you wrangling kids and dogs, getting youngsters on board when you train, with you going in and out of the house, may test you.

Here are some of the solutions I've seen those with children (especially younger children) employ:

1. Use Rewards!

Of course I was going to suggest this. We know that rewards can work for children, not just for dogs. I've seen parents reward their children for their involvement with the training with screen time or a trip to buy an ice cream or pizza for dinner.

I don't want to encourage bad habits in your children. You might train four or five times a week, which could end up being lots of treats! Rather than an ice cream every time, you might offer one reward for every two days of training.

2. Bake it into a Routine

We're all more likely to do difficult things when we form a routine. Pick a time when you think your child might be most amenable to this (you may need to combine this with #1!). Then stick to that time.

Always be prepped and ready to go before you involve the kids. That means camera set up, app at the ready, and training plan open.

3. Train with the Kids in the House

Training while someone else is in the house is still worthwhile. It might not be as useful as doing a session with the house empty but it's a good second best.

Consider training when the kids are in bed. This will be a closer approximation to an empty house. Remember that you're simply stepping to the other side of the front door, and you'll be monitoring everything that goes on inside. Take your baby monitor with you. Or better still, use the same camera type for your child's room as you use to watch your dog. That way you can use the same app on your phone to watch both.

If your children are teenagers, these strategies might be harder. The most common approach I see in these cases is training with the teens in the house.

Whatever you do, don't let kids being home be an excuse. I've seen families get their dogs over separation anxiety countless times, so I know it can be done.

Dealing with Reluctant Significant Others

Separation anxiety training ideally needs to be a team effort, so when it feels like you're flying solo, your frustration levels can mount. While you're right to want your significant other to participate equally, if they're not, training can still work.

Here are some tips:

1. Let it Go

You've got enough stress in your life without adding to it with arguments over separation anxiety training. Yes, it's better for the two of you to share the training, but you can still make progress if it's just you.

2. Highlight the Benefits (and the Risks)

Who wants to get off the sofa on a rainy Tuesday winter night to walk in and out of the front door over and over? No one, but the payoff is huge.

Your partner needs to know there's a risk that if they don't train, the result could be a dog who's fine when you leave, but not when they leave. You'll be the one with the freedom. They'll be the one who can't head out on a whim.

3. Ignore the Doubting

It could be that your partner's reluctance is driven by doubt in the process. They may think you should just be leaving your puppy to get on with it. Chances are, though, if you're reading this book you've tried that and it didn't work.

I've seen this discussion take place between couples so many times. The best way to counter the cynicism is just to get on and train. Let the results speak for themselves (even if by "results," we're talking about your puppy being able to do one minute rather than the one second he started on).

Can a Trainer Do the Training for You?

With regular dog training, this is an excellent approach for busy households. It's far better to hire someone to train your puppy if you don't have time than to not get the training done at all.

You typically have two options:

- Board and train, where you send your dog away, or

- Day training, where the trainer comes to you while you're out at work.

Unfortunately, neither of these are suited to separation anxiety training. Let's look at why.

Board and Train

It can seem like an obvious solution to your dog's separation anxiety: send your dog off to a trainer for two weeks and get his separation anxiety fixed.

As tempting as it sounds, board and train isn't the answer to separation anxiety. Here's why:

1. Separation Anxiety is Rarely, if Ever, Fixed in Just Two to Three Weeks

Separation anxiety is much more complicated than teaching a dog to sit or walk nicely on a leash. Fixing separation anxiety means changing a dog's emotion, not teaching him a new trick.

If anyone tells you they can fix your dog's separation anxiety in a matter of weeks, take that as a red flag.

2. Dogs Don't Generalize Well

We think that once a dog is over separation anxiety, he's over it. But dogs don't work like that. Change one thing and you change everything. A new location equals new fears.

This means that sending your dog away for separation anxiety training will be of no benefit when he comes back home. Even if he gets over separation anxiety in the trainer's location (but see #1; he likely won't), he still won't feel safe in your house. You'll still have to do the desensitization training.

3. Your Dog Might Be Left Alone in the Board and Train Facility

Can a board and train facility guarantee they will not leave your dog on his own, even for five minutes? Not being left alone is crucial to a dog with separation anxiety, as you know.

This rule is even more critical when in a new context. Even well-adjusted, non-anxious dogs can be upset by a new environment.

If you use board and train, have you looked your trainer in the eye and had them swear that your dog will not be left alone? And, just as importantly, have they guaranteed your dog will not be crated?

4. Board and Train Has Traditionally Meant Punishment-Based Training

Not all board and train professionals use punishment. Thankfully an increasing number of highly skilled, force-free trainers are now getting into board and train.

Hurting or scaring a dog into changing behavior isn't ethical, nor is it necessary. And in fact, it isn't even as effective as force-free training. There is no reason to use punishment to train, so don't believe any trainer who tells you it's the only or best way to train.

I often hear, though, "He came back from board and train a changed dog." If he had two weeks of punishment-based training, then what you're seeing isn't a calm dog: It's a shut-down dog who's decided the best way to avoid punishment is to not offer any behavior.

Treating fear with fear is not the way to fix separation anxiety.

5. There Are No Guarantees in Dog Training

Board and train, when done properly by a certified, force-free trainer, can bring about huge changes in your dog. But reputable trainers who do board and train offer no guarantees because they know it is unethical to do so.

There are no guarantees when working with dogs. If your board and train facility promises results, take that as a huge red, waving flag.

So, should you just skip the board and train if you have a dog who has separation anxiety?

Not necessarily. Don't send him away to work on his separation anxiety—but you could send him away for training on his jumping, reactivity to other dogs, dog play issues, and so on. Board and train can be very effective for lots of behaviors, just not separation anxiety!

Plus, having your dog stay somewhere else could be a problem-solver for you and your family. You might do it while you're on vacation or just when you need a break from his separation anxiety.

Before you book, ask the following questions:

- What training methods do you use? Look for words such as *force-free, positive reinforcement, humane, food, treats,* and *fun.* Words like *balanced, correction, leadership*, and *dominance* are code for trainers who use punishment.

- What exactly will happen to my dog when he gets it right? And when he gets it wrong?

- What's the training plan for him? (Ask to see this.)

- How are you going to work around his need to be with someone at all times?

If you get good answers to these questions, go ahead! If you have any doubt, trust your gut, move on, and find someone else.

Day Training

Board and train isn't right for separation anxiety, but day training might help. If your dog has a fear of being alone rather than a fear of being away from you, then someone else doing a bit of desensitization training could benefit.

I have two big reservations. First, you need to do a lot of repetitions when you're working on separation anxiety. You'll have to book an awful lot of sessions with a day trainer, and that's not going to be cheap.

Second, even if you decide to invest, there is a chance that your dog might end up being fine when your trainer does the leaving (because she's done all the desensitization), but not do well when you leave.

Choose a specialist separation anxiety trainer if you're going to hire someone. Most separation anxiety specialists work remotely and don't offer separation anxiety support as part of board and train or day training.

While I'm not dismissing either board and train or day training, they probably aren't your best bet for separation anxiety. If you are thinking of taking on a trainer, Chapter 1 includes some tips to help you make the hiring decision. You can find a list of trainers I have trained, my SA Pro Trainers ™, on the resources site (berightbackthebook.com).

Why We Need to Go Slow to Go Fast

As your training progresses and you begin to feel more confident with the process, it can be easy to push your puppy too hard. Many of us fall into one of two common traps: We're impatient, or we want to keep testing our puppy.

We're Impatient

As your training progresses you may feel tempted to take bigger jumps between your target durations. For example, say your puppy has aced every target duration for the last five sessions but you've only been going up in one-minute increments. You want to now try going up by five minutes. This could work, but there's also a risk that it might push your puppy too far too fast.

It's like climbing a ladder up a cliff. The safest way to get to the top is just to take it rung-by-rung. The rungs are close together, so it does take you many steps. However, if you decide to do three, four, or five rungs at a time, or jump and grasp the highest rung you can reach, there's a risk you'll slip and fall.

And when you fall it will be all the way down again.

Now, that's not to say that jumping up in five-minute steps when you previously were doing one-minute steps will cause your puppy to go all the way back to square one. But there is a danger that by pushing your puppy too far your progress will stall.

By speeding up, we risk making things worse and hampering our progress. If we'd have stuck with the step-by-step approach, we'd have fared better. It's often the case with separation anxiety training that we have to slow down to go fast.

We Want to Keep Testing Our Puppy

Another temptation is going out and running the clock just to see how your puppy does. You wait until you see your puppy starting to get distressed. You note the time and use that as your next duration.

The problem is, though, that in that moment of your puppy getting distressed, you have just given him an experience of being alone not being safe.

Doing a baseline is a form of testing a puppy too. To do this well you must be cautious and return on the "a" of anxious.

Get this wrong and it's like jumping up the ladder only to miss the rung you grasp for.

I used to encourage baseline testing frequently, because that's how everyone did it. But now I don't, because as we've explored elsewhere in this book, it's never a good idea to allow a puppy or dog to go over threshold.

Until recently most trainers thought that we needed to see the fear response "in action" to assess the severity of the dog's condition. Some trainers still believe this to be necessary. Can you imagine going to see a therapist because you had a debilitating fear of spiders only to hear her say that, before she can treat you, she needs to see how afraid of spiders you really are? She then proceeds to lead you into a room of spiders to assess how you react.

A good trainer can assess your puppy without causing your puppy any more distress—and we can do so without risking your puppy slipping down the ladder of progress.

Do Puppies Ever Really "Just Get over It"?

A final word on how we approach getting a puppy over separation anxiety. You might have had friends tell you that their dog had separation anxiety, but they didn't do any of this "silly" training, and that their dog "just got over it."

Is this ever the case? It might be. If their puppy wasn't frightened of being home alone but was just bored or frustrated then, yes, just leaving the puppy to get over it might have worked.

And it can, in some instances work for scared puppies too. Here's how: The puppy is left to deal with the thing that frightens him at full intensity; that is, he has a long absence he can't cope with. This might be repeated such that the puppy has multiple scary alone-time experiences. Sometimes this results in puppies who seem to come out the other side of the fear. It's a technique that's known as *flooding*.

Flooding is actually an approach used with human patients. The patient is exposed to the fear-inducing stimulus at full intensity but then, having experienced the fear and survived, is able to process that the thing they feared did not kill them and they did get through it.

Flooding is a form of exposure therapy (face-the-fear treatment), but rather than gradual exposure it's full-intensity exposure.

Before undertaking flooding therapy, human patients are told that:

1. It will be traumatic, and

2. It might not work.

They can then make an informed choice as to whether they wish to proceed. But here are the issues with dogs:

1. It will be traumatic, and

2. It might not work, but

3. We cannot get their consent.

If dogs are put through flooding treatment, they have no idea that it's anything but real. So they'll experience a petrifying situation over which they have no control and that they can't consent to.

On top of that, human studies show flooding often doesn't work. With dogs, more often than not flooding makes things worse, simply because they aren't able to process that this was "just therapy."

Back to those dogs who seemed to have just got over it: There's no doubt in my mind that many of these dogs were flooded. Not intentionally. Owners aren't told that's what they are doing when they leave their dogs to get on with it. Nonetheless, some of these dogs may have recovered, but not without some horrifying experiences.

The bottom line is that flooding, or leaving a puppy to get on with it, is risky, inhumane, and unethical. So, let's just stick to humane gradual exposure training and ignore anyone who suggests otherwise.

Anxiety Medication for Your Puppy

The gold-standard treatment for dog separation anxiety is the training I've outlined together with anxiety medication. Anxiety medication for puppies? Yes, puppies do go on medication for their fear-based issues.

In fact, some vets and vet behaviorists would argue that, as young brains develop, that's exactly the time to consider medication to help those brains develop appropriately. The last thing we want is for a puppy to have fear imprinted on his young brain. Without help that fear might stay in the dog's brain for life. That's why I advise you to discuss medication early.

You might encounter some reluctance. Many hold a firm view that puppies under six months shouldn't be medicated, so don't be surprised if your vet says no. You can always seek a second opinion.

If your vet does agree to anxiety medications, what can you

expect? I've seen hundreds of dogs who have separation anxiety go on medication, and these are the ones I see most commonly:

Antidepressants/Anti-Anxiety Classes of Medication

These include:

- SSRIs, such a fluoxetine and paroxetine;

- TCAs, including clomipramine; and

- MAOs, such as selgiline.

Both fluoxetine and clomipramine are available in dog-specific formats (Reconcile and Clomicalm, respectively). However, certainly in the case of fluoxetine, vets tend to prescribe the generic version. Clomicalm is more often prescribed than clomipramine, though (as of 2019) clomipramine is now recognized as approved for use for dogs by the FDA in the United States.

These medications are given daily to your puppy and take some time to build up (usually a few weeks to a few months). These are sometimes called *standing* medications.

Situational Anxiolytic Meds

These are typically given before a particularly stressful event, such as a visit to the vet, a thunderstorm, or whatever event the dog finds fear-inducing.

These medications could include:

- Benzodiazepines,

- Clonidine,

- Trazodone, and

- Gabapentin.

A Combination of Standing Medications and Situational Medications

The first medication your dog goes on might not make any difference to their anxiety. You might decide to change the dosage or use a combination of anxiety medications. This could include:

1. Starting with standing medications and working on the dosage to get the minimum effective dosage for any given dog.

2. If the desired result isn't achieved with just one medication despite dosage adjustments, then the standing medication might be combined with the situational medication.

3. Changing the standing medication altogether, either to another medication within the same class or to a medication in a different class.

Brain chemistry is complicated (understatement) and there are more than 40 different medications that help to change brain chemistry. No wonder, then, that the process to find the right med (or meds), at the right dosage, and in the right combination can be a protracted one.

That's why I'm so passionate about considering anxiety medications early and often. I certainly wish I hadn't been so resistant to put my own puppy on medication. I think my—and especially his—quality of life would have benefited. I resisted putting Percy on anxiety medication and insisted on trying anything and everything else first. I really did see medication as a "last resort." But anxiety medication is humane and for an anxious dog provides a huge boost for their quality of life. I guarantee that if you're reluctant about anxiety medication and feeling skeptical, or that it's not right, I was more reluctant and more skeptical than you are! It was a gamechanger for Percy and for his training, and I have no regrets whatsoever (other than maybe wishing I hadn't been so stubborn!).

Unless your vet advises that there are medical reasons why your puppy can't go on anxiety medication, you should see it as a first resort, just like insulin for a person who has diabetes.

FAQs about Anxiety Medications

These are some of the most common questions about anxiety medications. (Questions I too once had!)

Will it Change My Puppy's Personality?

You're worried that your bouncy, goofy puppy will become a hollow, characterless version of themselves. The truth is, you've been watching too many movies like *One Flew Over the Cuckoo's Nest*. When vets prescribe anxiety medications, they aren't trying to suppress your dog's personality. In fact, their goal is to reduce your puppy's anxiety so that your puppy's personality comes to the fore. Your happy, silly puppy's true self shines through as their anxious side fades. Your puppy gets to be the best version of himself.

Will I Get a Zombie Puppy?

Medications for anxiety or depression aren't used to create a flat, grayed-out version of the patient. True, they do change the patient,

❚❚ The right medication at the right dosage will not turn your puppy into a zombie.

but in a positive way, by allowing the patient's non-anxious personality to be seen. There are likely plenty of people in your life who are on anxiety medication without you realizing: healthy, functioning people who aren't zombies but who are instead coping better with life.

The right medication at the right dosage will not turn your puppy into a zombie.

I'm in a Country where Vets Don't Prescribe Anxiety Meds. What Can I Do?

It can seem like vets only prescribe anxiety medication for dogs in certain countries. You might think you don't live in one of those countries. In my experience, there are plenty of places in the world where vets will prescribe anxiety medications for dogs. This is especially so in Australia, Canada, the UK, and the United States. It's often the case that the decision to medicate differs as much among vets within a country as it does among countries. If you find that your vet is reluctant to consider anxiety medication, you have three main options. You can:

- Do your research, present articles on medication for anxiety that you've read, and hope that will sway your vet.

- Ask around to see if you can find a vet who is more pro–anxiety medications for dogs. It's perfectly OK to ask for a second opinion. Remember that all you're doing is being your puppy's best advocate.

- Ask to be referred to a vet behaviorist.

If there are no vets in your area who work with dogs and anxiety medication, then ask if there is a vet behaviorist you could work with. A vet behaviorist specializes in the use of medication for behavior change.

How Long Will My Puppy Be on Medication?

The answer is this will vary considerably from dog to dog. Your puppy might need to be on anxiety medication only as long as you work through separation anxiety. Other dogs might need to remain on anxiety medications even after the separation anxiety seems to have been resolved.

You might be concerned about your puppy being on medication long-term either because of the cost implications or because you worry about side effects. It's true that the cost of anxiety medications is not negligible, especially if you are already feeling the pinch from the money you spend on daycare costs, dog walkers, pet sitters, and cameras.

If cost is the issue, ask your vet how you can reduce the cost of the prescription. This could include getting a prescription for a generic version of the medication or asking the vet if you can fill the prescription at a regular pharmacy. Also check whether your insurance will cover anxiety medication.

If the side effects bother you, then do your research on Google Scholar, check the manufacturer sites, and quiz your vet. Do not get your information about anxiety medication side effects from online forums or Facebook groups.

But if you can't countenance your puppy being on medications for life, don't think about how long. Just think about your puppy being on medication while you work through separation anxiety training. Once you get your puppy to a place where he seems less upset with you leaving, then have another conversation with your vet about weaning him off.

Are the Side Effects Dangerous?

This is absolutely a conversation you must have with your vet if you have any concerns whatsoever. What I hear from vets is that the side effect profile for anxiety medications is low and that many dogs can be on these medications for life without any problems.

You'll notice side effects (if there are any for your dog) during the first few weeks of your puppy being on a new medication. Ask your vet for the specific side effects to look for. That way you're not assuming that any change you see in your puppy during that time is automatically due to the medication.

If you find your puppy has changed in a way that you're uncomfortable with, speak with your vet. Side effects should wear off in those first few weeks, but if they don't, or if they are severe, your vet might change the dosage or even the medication.

How Do I Know Medications Are Working?

The major indicator is your training progress improving. If you're not doing home-alone training, then you're looking for changes such as:

- A reduction in following around the house,

- Less interest in you and what you're doing, and

- Being able to close doors such as the bathroom or bedroom without your puppy losing it.

Questions to Ask Yourself about Your Preparedness for Anxiety Medications

It's time to talk about the things you need to ask *yourself* before you decide to medicate your dog. This is a big decision for owners.

As an owner who was initially reluctant to put my dog on anxiety medications but was thrilled with the results when I did, if I had to do this over again, knowing everything that I know now, these are the questions I would ask myself:

- Am I ready to do the training?

- Am I prepared to deal with the consequences of the medication not making a difference?

- Can I handle the judgment?

- Am I okay with the expense?

- Have I done enough to quell my concerns?

Am I Ready to Do the Training?

If you are putting your dog on medication, you will get the best outcome if you also put time into the training. Medication is a part of the solution, not the whole solution. However, there are some circumstances in which medicating without training is an acceptable option. If your dog responds well to short-term anxiety medications, you could use the medications when you have to leave but can't get anyone to stay with him. The anxiety meds may mean that, even though he's on his own for an hour or so, he won't go over threshold.

A word of caution: Always test the medication first to see if it has the desired effect. Some dogs will still get very upset when they're left. In those cases, I always say to video your dog and be ready to come back if the meds aren't working.

Am I Prepared to Deal with the Consequences of the Medication Not Making a Difference?

In other words, what if the medications don't work? For a good number of dogs, an anxiety medication will make a difference to their home-alone issues—but not for 100% of dogs. The reality is that for many dogs it can take time to get the right anxiety medication at the right dose. And it might even require a combination of medications.

There are more than 40 medications that are prescribed as psychotropic medications in humans (medications that act on the brain's neurotransmitters). What exactly causes each condition is evolving, so it's rare to get the right med at the right dose on the first try for humans. If dopamine deficiency is causing the issue, for example, a medication that works on serotonin levels won't do the job.

The issue is no less challenging with dogs.

When you work with a vet or vet behaviorist, most likely they'll prescribe one anxiety medication to start with. You'll be asked to monitor your dog for changes (good and bad). If you don't see any significant improvement, their next move will probably be to adjust the dosage of that medication. In fact, they may adjust the dosage several times. It depends on the starting dosage and increments.

If you still don't see an improvement in training, your vet might decide that it's not the right medication. Or they might decide to keep your dog on that original medication but now add a second, or sometimes a third, medication. This combination therapy approach is common in human patients, and I see it being used increasingly for dogs.

But this still might not get you there, even with more dosage adjustments. Your vet might then consider changing the medications. And once again you might go through a series of dosage adjustments.

All of this does take time (all the more reason for starting medication early), but the payoff is worth it as you see your training outcomes start to improve.

However, the process doesn't work for all dogs. With some dogs it seems, no matter what medication or medications the vet decides to use, the dog's brain doesn't respond to them. This is hard enough for most owners but if you are someone who was reluctant to medicate your dog or you had friends and family who were skeptical, this will hit you especially hard.

If it's that hard to find the right medication to treat an anxious dog, should you even bother trying? The answer is yes. Yes, absolutely. Because when they work, you stand a really good chance of transforming your training.

Can I Handle the Judgment?

If others judge you about your dog's treatment, don't feel surprised, and try not to get upset. Remember that other people are not in your shoes. You're making a decision to help your dog feel better. You're trying to improve your dog's quality of life. Don't let anyone judge you for doing your best for your dog.

Am I Okay with the Expense?

Prescription anxiety medications aren't always cheap—but they are usually a lot cheaper than the separation anxiety "remedies" you can buy online. They are also cheaper than replacing doors or taking a dog to the vet when they've torn a nail. Consider the cost of the drugs in that context.

For some dogs, you might be looking at quite a long-term prescription, but for others, it might not be. It depends on the dog.

Have I Done Enough to Quell My Concerns?

Ultimately, you're the one making this decision. You're the one who needs to defend this decision if you get challenged, so how informed are you?

If you're worried about side effects, have you done enough research and had your own questions answered so that you feel comfortable with the choice you are making? There's a lot of great information out there. The more research I do, the more comfortable I am with medication for anxious dogs. When researching, use Google Scholar. There's so much misinformation and scaremongering online. You don't need sensationalism. You need solid facts. Google Scholar is the place for facts.

As for side effects, dogs and people have taken these medications for years. Significant side effects are rare. In my mind, dry mouth is less of a medical concern than a ripped nail or the anxiety of barking for eight hours non-stop.

It's a welfare issue. I want my dogs to have a good quality of life and to live as long as possible, which is why I opt for treatments that are safe, tested, and known to be effective.

What *Not* to Ask

As a final thought, here's a question I don't want you to ask yourself: "Have I exhausted all other options?" I often hear people say, "I put them on meds because it was a last resort." Anxiety medication should be one of our first treatment options for separation anxiety, not one of the last.

But many of us (me included) prefer to try so-called natural remedies first. It's easy to get drawn in by the marketing and they seem to offer only upsides. No wonder we want to try these first.

Remember that anything that changes a being's chemistry or biology has side effects. To put it another way, if there are no side effects, it's not having any effect. So, don't be fooled by remedies that claim to change the dog's brain without any side effects.

Unfortunately, way too many of these treatments are out there.

Compared to anxiety medications, natural or complementary remedies:

- Aren't as rigorously tested,

- Aren't as proven,

- Can cost more, and

- Can be marketed much more aggressively, making us think that they're the better choice.

I'm also skeptical about companies that seem to brand themselves as natural, ethical, small businesses—and hence in stark contrast to big pharma—but that are, in fact, owned by larger, less-ethical corporations. CBD oil is a great example of this in practice. Some seemingly independent CBD oil companies are owned by tobacco and beverage companies. (We'll talk more about CBD oil in the "CBD Oil" section later in this chapter.)

While we're busy trying those different approaches, not only does our bank account suffer, but we delay the treatment that is most likely to make a difference for our dog.

Whether or not you decide to put your puppy on anxiety medication, do your homework and ask the right questions. That way, you'll know you're going into this as informed as you can be.

How to Ask Your Vet for Help with Anxiety Medication

If you've decided you want to put your puppy on anxiety medication to help the training, you obviously want your vet on board. Here are some suggestions for broaching the subject (assuming your vet doesn't mention it first).

Initial conversation about anxiety medications:
"I've been researching separation anxiety and it seems that many dogs respond well to a combination of training and anxiety medications. Is this something you can help with?"

If your vet is reluctant and sees medication as a last resort:
"I can understand why you would suggest we try other

alternatives first, but it seems like anxiety medications really help some dogs, so I'd like to start there first. If anxiety medications don't work, I'd be happy to try other alternatives after that."

If your vet still says no, you can always seek a second opinion.

If medication doesn't seem to be working:

"It's been several weeks now and we're just not seeing any improvement. What are our options?"

Should You Take a More "Natural" Approach Instead?

Let's be clear: Natural doesn't always mean better. And it doesn't always mean safe.

Look at COVID-19. The virus is natural. The vaccine is produced in a lab. Most of us think taking the manufactured vaccine is preferable to being exposed to the naturally occurring coronavirus.

I do understand why so many owners like to explore so-called alternative treatments for dogs. We want the best for our dogs, and all of us can slip into thinking that natural must mean better. However, I've had almost no success with natural supplements with the hundreds of client dogs I've worked with, nor have the hundreds of owners who've read my first book or joined my groups.

These are my concerns with natural remedies:

- I've not seen the magical results so many products claim.

- They aren't cheap, and I worry that owners get lured into

wasting precious money and time on products that won't help.

- Natural isn't always good. It's human nature to hold the (false) idea that whatever is natural cannot be wrong. Philosophers call this the "appeal to nature fallacy."

- There is no evidence to support the claims of the vast majority of natural cures touted for separation anxiety.

Cyanide, arsenic, asbestos, mercury, and lead are all natural—yet all of these can kill us. For a dog, chocolate can be a killer. In fact, the purer the chocolate and the higher the cocoa content, the more lethal it is to dogs.

Dogs are natural scavengers and will get into all sorts of things they mustn't, but we know scarfing the garbage isn't good for them. When it comes to natural products for dogs, instead of saying, "It's natural, so it must be good," we should ask, "It's natural, but is it any good?"

Let's look at the most common alternative therapies for treating separation anxiety.

Supplements

You can buy a number of products over the counter that contain supplements purporting to help alleviate separation anxiety. The most common supplements include:

L-Theanine. This amino acid is derived from green tea. Research in both humans and dogs is limited but suggests it could be safe and may help.

Alpha-casozepine. This is a protein found in cow's milk. You can find it in a number of products. One study in dogs determined it to be as equally effective as selegiline in reducing anxiety in dogs. But again, there isn't a lot of research.

L-tryptophan. Tryptophan does have a link to serotonin and is an essential amino acid found in turkey. Research about the benefits isn't conclusive.

Pheromones

Dog-appeasing pheromones are intended to simulate the pheromones released by a lactating mother. Pheromone-based products include diffusers, sprays, and collars. Some research has been promising, though effectiveness is significantly impacted by following the precise instructions for use. Sadly, other research suggests that they might not be effective at all.

Some owners report success with pheromones. Others say they see no difference.

Wraps and Pressure Vests

There are a wide range of wraps and pressure vests on the market that all purport to calm your dog by applying pressure to their body. I've not seen these have much effect on dogs, but some people say they see benefits.

Many of these products come with a 100% money-back guarantee, so you can always try them if you're curious.

CBD Oil

CBD is derived from the cannabis plant. It contains less than 0.3% of the THC compound, which is responsible for making users feel high.

THC itself can be lethal to dogs in small quantities. Though there is limited research on the use of CBD for pets, initial findings look promising for epilepsy and arthritis. It may be some time before we know whether CDB works for separation anxiety and at what dosage.

Lack of Testing and Regulation

On top of the logic fail that we're all guilty of that "natural equals good," my other concerns about alternative treatments are these:

- Some natural products require less testing than prescription medications, and manufacturers don't always need research to back up their claims. Many are sold as food supplements, so they don't require the rigorous approval process that prescription medications do.

- Prescription medications may get a bad rap, but pharmaceutical companies do have to prove the claims they make.

- Sourcing a consistent product can be a challenge. This is especially true of CBD oil. Many owners have reported to me that finding a brand they trust can be problematic. It's not like when you buy ibuprofen. No matter where you get it from, the ibuprofen is the same product—and the pill in your hand has gone through specific testing.

If you want to explore alternative treatments, do so knowing that many claims are untested. Always do your research and do inform your vet.

Ideas for Giving Pills to Dogs

If you've opted for anxiety medication, you need to work out how to give your puppy medication every day.

You can teach a dog to be fine with taking a pill—but it takes time and training. If you force him to take his tablet, he'll quickly get wise to you and start doing his utmost to avoid pill time.

Since training a dog to take a pill takes time, most of us opt for masking the pill or capsule in food.

Following are some options for hiding the pill in food. Put the pill straight into:

- Hot dogs,
- Sausages,
- Burgers,
- Marshmallows,
- Cheese slices,
- Cheese paste,
- Pate,
- Ham or turkey slices, or
- Chicken hearts.

Put the pill in a slurry made with:

- Cat food,
- Tripe,
- Fish,
- Peanut butter,
- Molasses,
- Liver, or
- Anything strong-tasting.

Coat the pill in:

- Raw liver, fish, or tripe gloop,

- For dogs who aren't dairy-sensitive, butter or cream cheese, or

- Dog-friendly peanut butter. (Make sure it doesn't contain xylitol!)

Note: Check with your vet or pharmacist whether it's okay to split or crush a tablet, or whether it's okay to open a capsule.

When Your Dog Resists Medications

Dogs have very sensitive tastebuds and will detect the bitter taste of medication in whatever you give them if you're not careful. Do it once and they might associate any pill-giving with a nasty taste. That's what's happening if your puppy is avoiding you when you approach with a pill.

To overcome this:

1. Change the food you use to mask the pill.

2. Vary the way you deliver the pill so that your approaching your puppy with the food in your hand at a certain time of day doesn't tip him off that you are giving him a pill.

   - Make it a game: Toss the coated pill for your puppy to catch, or hide the coated pill for your puppy to find.

   - Use the coated pill as reward for quick-fire training (touch, watch me, look at that, etc.).

- Use a 1-2-3 punch. For example,
  for a cheese-coated pill:

  » Give one piece of cheese with no pill.

  » Don't give the dog time to chew
    before you quickly offer the second
    piece of cheese *with* the pill.

  » Give the third piece of cheese,
    with no pill, right away.

- Give each piece almost before they've had
  a chance to finish the previous one.

- Involve other household dogs (if you have
  them) to make it competitive and urgent.

- Get other family members to give the pill.

- Give the pill as a reward on walks.

- Drop the pill on walks for your puppy to "find."

Don't use the same routine. Mix up the time, place (different room, outside, on walks), who gives the food/pill, and where the food comes from (sometimes freezer, fridge, cupboard, etc.). Keep mixing it up so that he can't pick up clues. For a really suspicious puppy, mix it up every time.

Vet Clinic Visits

Regardless of whether you are considering anxiety medication for your puppy, you should make an appointment with your vet to discuss your puppy's conditions.

Vet appointments—especially those involving treatment requiring a stay at the clinic—can be scary for any animal, let alone a puppy who has separation anxiety.

Luckily, there are ways to alleviate some of the stress of these visits. First, let's step back and understand the challenge.

Why Do Dogs Who Have Separation Anxiety Struggle at the Vet?

Dogs who have separation anxiety fear two things the most: being alone and being crated. Vet clinic visits and stays create a perfect storm of both. Dogs are occasionally left alone as they wait for treatment, have tests, or recover from treatments, and it's common to crate them as they wake up from sedatives or anesthetics.

> Your goal is to make vet visits fear-free.

Dogs who have separation anxiety often get worse when they've had fear-inducing, over-threshold experiences. I've seen plenty of dogs return from vet stays with significant regressions in their separation anxiety training.

Even if your puppy isn't required to stay at the vet clinic, the vet team may want to take your puppy out of the exam room for treatment or tests, and this can be upsetting for some puppies.

Make Vet Visits Less Stressful

Vet stays are unavoidable, so what can you do to make them less stressful for your puppy? Your goal is to make vet visits fear-free and so you want to understand what your vet can do to help achieve this. Here are a few ideas:

- Have a thorough discussion with your vet well before the appointment.

- Break pre-procedure testing, treatment, and recuperation into steps.

- Ask about anxiety medications for your puppy's visits.

- Clarify whether your puppy will be alone at any point.

- See if your vet can avoid using a crate.

- Ask how quickly you can take your puppy home.

Have a Thorough Discussion with Your Vet Well before the Appointment

Letting your vet know about your puppy's separation anxiety is key. Not only can they help provide excellent advice about how to treat separation anxiety, they can also work with their team to limit the amount of isolation and crating your puppy experiences during any given visit.

Break Pre-Procedure Testing, Treatment, and Recuperation into Steps

One of the main reasons your dog will be isolated is that blood tests, samples, X-rays, and so forth can be done more efficiently if veterinary staff can take the dog and perform those procedures according to their schedule. This may mean a great deal of waiting solo for your puppy.

If the treatment is elective/non-urgent, ask your veterinary clinic if the procedures can be split into smaller, one-off appointments. Another option is to see if the clinic can condense procedures into a shorter window and do them all while you wait in the reception area, ready to take your puppy home as soon as possible. Another alternative is to ask if you can wait with your puppy in an empty exam room or in your car until they are ready to see him.

Ask about Anxiety Medications for Your Puppy's Visits

Giving your puppy a short-acting anxiety medication may help alleviate some of his panic, leading to a smoother vet visit. The sedatives your vet will give you for home use are typically given orally. The dose can be timed in advance of the appointment. (These same types of medications are often prescribed to people who have a fear of flying or a fear of the dentist.)

For surgery itself, ask your vet about pre-anesthesia sedation. Ask if you can stay with your puppy while he's being sedated. Once he's more settled, you can leave him in the capable hands of the vet and vet techs.

Clarify whether Your Puppy Will Be Alone at Any Point

Your anxious puppy is most likely to panic when he's left alone without sedation and not under full anesthesia. Clarify whether he'll be left alone at any point and ask if someone could be around for those times. Even a vet tech writing cases notes nearby would help.

See if Your Vet Can Avoid Using a Crate

Crating is often used for safety purposes, when your groggy puppy wakes from sedation or anesthesia. Depending on the procedure your puppy required, your vet may be open to keeping him out of the crate, so it's worth asking.

Ask How Quickly You Can Take Your Puppy Home

Some vets will prioritize discharging an anxious patient. They'll let you take him home as soon as it's safe to do so, rather than waiting until the end of the practice day.

What if It's an Emergency?

Of course, if it's an emergency, most of these practices are not possible. In all cases, the emergency must take precedence over your puppy's anxiety, but you can still inquire about recovery and timing to help with the transition post-emergency.

Physical and Mental Health: Not "Either/Or"

A growing number of vets are beginning to understand the impact of a fear-filled vet visit. These vets are committed to doing what they can to make your puppy's visit more bearable.

Remember: Your puppy's physical health is vital to his mental well-being. While his anxiety does matter, don't let it prevent you from booking those much-needed vet appointments!

Crate Rest for a Crate-Phobic Puppy

Your puppy is likely to have surgery at some point. With recovery, crating is typically advised. However, it might be that no matter what you do your puppy just isn't okay with the crate, so what can you do?

Crate rest is typically advised to prevent movement and hence aid surgical or orthopedic recovery. If your puppy hates his crate,

crate rest won't achieve that goal. Rather than be still in his crate, he's likely to be frantic.

With the goal of limiting movement in mind you can:

- Have your puppy next to you when you work or watch TV. If you're worried about him wandering around, either tether him to you (use a harness to connect a leash and tie the leash around your waist) or have an exercise pen around both of you (sounds crazy but it works).

    - If you live with family, take turns having the puppy next to you.

    - If you live alone, see if you can draft in help from friends or a paid sitter. When my dogs were puppies, I had support from my two beautiful nieces, Charlotte and Becca. "Come sit with my puppy" didn't seem to be too difficult a sell!

- When you can't tether or sit with your puppy, try using an exercise pen rather than using a crate. Feed them in their pen or, if dinner is finished, give them a yummy puppy-friendly chew to work on.

- If all else fails and there are times when you just have to crate, speak to your vet about medications to help your puppy cope with the confinement.

Chapter Takeaways

- 🐾 Gradual exposure is the tried-and-true method that will help you get your puppy over separation anxiety.

- 🐾 Gradual exposure training might take time and a lot of effort, but it's the absolute best method for getting a puppy you can happily leave.

- 🐾 Training progression is never a straight line, so expect ups and downs.

- 🐾 Recovery is best achieved via a combination of training and anxiety medication.

- 🐾 Despite what people tell you, your puppy won't just get over a fear of being alone. Training is the way to go.

It always seems impossible until it's done.

NELSON MANDELA

CHAPTER 5

Separation Anxiety Training Mindset

Separation anxiety training isn't just about how your puppy responds to that challenge. The outlook we have and how we handle the ups and downs is often the biggest factor in getting our puppy over separation anxiety.

In this chapter we explore why not going through this journey alone is so important. We look at how habits can help us stick with training. There is also information on what to do when training falters and how to set realistic expectations for your training and your puppy. We also review what to do when this all feels like it's too much. Finally, we consider how best to handle judgment and guilt.

Community Matters

When my dog Percy had separation anxiety, my husband and I felt incredibly isolated. Not only did we have a dog we couldn't leave, which cut us off from our social life, we also felt alone because whenever we tried to talk to anyone, they just didn't get it.

Instead of going it alone, connect with other owners facing the same challenges. In this highly networked world, there are many ways to reach out to people who are experiencing what you're going through.

Here's why teaming up will help you:

- Separation anxiety training is simple, but it isn't easy.

- Teaching is the best way to learn.

- Sharing stories lightens the load.

- You can team up with accountability buddies.

- Communities are pivotal to good habits.

- You can get help with the basics.

- You simply know you're not the only one.

Separation Anxiety Training Is Simple, but it Isn't Easy

When done properly, separation anxiety training using desensitization has an excellent track record. However, there are going to be times when you think you will never get there. Chatting with other owners who are working on the process—especially when you're stuck—will remind you of the highs, not just the lows. If you have an active group around you, there's a strong chance one of them will be up when you're down. You, in turn, can support others through their dips.

Teaching Is the Best Way to Learn

Even though it's a straightforward process, the training method has many moving parts. One area for which you might benefit from input is reading your dog's body language. Another pair of eyes on your dog may help you see something you're missing. And you can reciprocate. You'll likely get better at reading your dog by helping others assess their dogs.

Sharing Stories Lightens the Load

Separation anxiety is undoubtedly a serious topic, though it does have its lighter side. If you think about it, we owners do some odd things:

- Exercises where you go in and out of the front door 15 times—even without a coat in the winter—because you haven't reached the "put coat on" training step yet.

- Standing in the street and listening for your dog, while whispering to your neighbor that everything is okay but that you can't chat right now because you're trying to hear what your dog is doing.

- Sitting in a coffee shop and Skyping your home laptop so you can spy on your dog. (Who Skypes themselves, people?)

- Getting so excited about seeing your dog sleeping that you share screen grabs with your friends. "Look, I just went out, and he slept the whole way through.

ERMAHGERD!" If your friends are anything like most people's, they politely indulge you while at the same time thinking, "Uh, it's just a sleeping dog. Get over it!"

In the midst of separation anxiety, all of this is routine. But no one else you know will understand. If you've done any of the above, you need to connect with other owners of dogs who have separation anxiety because they *will* understand.

You Can Team Up with Accountability Buddies

Having goals and getting others to hold you accountable to those goals helps enormously. "How long will it take?" is the one question everyone asks. What I love about connecting owners is that this becomes less important than "How's my dog progressing?"

It's not that it isn't important to know how long it might take for the challenging stuff to end, of course. It's just that I see owners go through a refreshing change in which they start to become motivated by progress and not by "Is this over yet?" syndrome.

By having a support network, you can embrace the notion that celebrating the small successes along the way motivates you to get to your end goal. It's the same with any behavior change, like going to the gym, losing weight, or learning a new language.

Communities Are Pivotal to Good Habits

Separation anxiety training is best done little and often. This means you must get into the habit. Much has been written about how habits form, but community and accountability are big factors. We're more likely to do something if the people around us are doing the same thing. We're more likely to stick with a new behavior if others we know hold us accountable.

Join a group of people going through the same training process. The owners I work with all get access to a membership club and private forum in which they share their progress, have a space to vent, and connect with people going through the same thing.

Even if your community isn't specifically for separation anxiety, find buddies to help you stick to your training schedule. Share your plan and get them to keep you on track when you're struggling.

You Can Get Help with the Basics

Even if your separation anxiety group is an online community, they can still assist with practical, local matters. Take managing absences. There will be times when you are in a bind. Perhaps something unexpected comes up or maybe a sitter cancels. See if your online community can help.

The internet shrinks the concept of six degrees of separation. Even if you're in Tampa and they're in Toronto, they may know someone who knows someone. Or they may have some brilliantly creative idea you've never thought of. Or—who knows—maybe someone in your online group is close enough to jump in and help.

You Simply Know You're Not the Only One

It can feel like you're the only person with a dog who has separation anxiety, but when you join a group, you'll be astonished by how many other people are going through the same thing.

How Habits Help Our Training

When a new behavior becomes a habit, we're more likely to stick with it. It becomes part of our routine, and we do it without thinking. Habits are a powerful ingredient for behavior change.

You may have heard it takes about three weeks for a new behavior to become a habit. Actually, there's no evidence for the magic number of 21 days. In fact, research by University College, London, shows it takes longer—about 70 days or more. This matters because we get impatient and expect new ways of doing things to become habits far quicker than we should. If we expect something to start feeling easier after three weeks and it doesn't, we might be disappointed. We need to give behavior change at least two months before it gets truly sticky.

Willpower is pretty puny, the research shows. Willpower isn't enough to get us through difficult change. When we make that change a habit though, we're more likely to stick with it.

Studies show that they are several key elements to habit formation. These include:

- Use "cue and reward,"

- Make it easy,

- Track your progress,

- Recognize your excuses,

- Be kind to yourself, and

- Focus on the process, not the outcome.

Let's look at how each of those relate to separation anxiety training.

Use "Cue and Reward"

Cues and rewards help us develop habits. Having a cue prompts your brain: It's time to do that thing. Your cue might be "Do the training before we cook dinner." You do the training every night at the same time, just before dinner, and prepping dinner becomes the cue.

Rewards help because our brains are programmed to respond to rewards. But the challenge is we are programmed to value immediate rewards, not rewards that we might get in a few weeks, months, or years. That's what makes saving for retirement or going to the gym so difficult: It takes a long time before we get a payback.

The same is true with separation anxiety. We put a lot of effort in now, but the reward of being able to leave our dog for any length of time often comes much later. To stay motivated with training we use short-term rewards. Here are some suggestions I use with clients:

Immediately After Training

- Indulge in a sweet treat.

- Stream an episode of your favorite show (say you'll watch it after you train).

- Do something mindless like surf YouTube or Facebook.

- And while you're on Facebook, do something meaningful, like share your successes with your owner peers and let them congratulate you.

- Take a long, hot bath.

- Pour a glass of wine.

- You decide!

At the End of a Week of Training

- Buy that top you've been eyeing.

- Go out to eat (either somewhere you can take your dog, or arrange a sitter).

- Get a dog sitter and go see a movie.

- Book a massage or a spa trip.

- Arrange a sitter just so you can do something you've been missing doing.

- You decide!

Make it Easy

If you make the process as easy as you can and remove obstacles, then you're more likely to do what you said you'd do. For example, one study showed that gym-goers who lived closer to a gym were more likely to go than those who lived one and a half miles farther away. Another study suggested that if the gym is on your direct route to work then you're more likely to go.

Ease can also make us fall into bad habits. Think about how much more likely you are to eat chocolate if it's left on the counter than if it's put away in a cupboard. Or how easy Netflix makes it for you to watch the next episode of your favorite series by auto-playing it.

Being lazy makes sense from an evolutionary perspective. When you're hunting for food and calories are hard to come by, taking shortcuts makes sense. Doing anything that requires effort doesn't.

With separation anxiety training, reducing the effort you need to put into it might mean buying a dedicated webcam you leave set up or always having your training plan printed out and handy.

Owners who work with me use my separation anxiety training app. It generates plans, has space for them to record progress, and even has a stopwatch. It's designed to make things easy.

Track Your Progress

By charting progress, you'll see how far you've come even when you feel stuck. Log your training to help you see progress. Regularly review your training records to remind yourself how far you've come. The app my owners use is packed with options for tracking and recording progress, which are presented visually. Nothing beats seeing your dog's upward progress on a beautiful chart.

You don't need an app to do this, though. You can create simple charts in any spreadsheet software.

Recognize Your Excuses

It's easy to use the same reasons not to do something. There's always something else we could do. But experts tell us that if we start to spot our pattern of excuse-making, we can reduce the power of those excuses.

Be Kind to Yourself

Self-criticism kills motivation. Our critical inner voice can easily crush our enthusiasm. So what if you think you should have started separation anxiety training months ago? And who cares if you don't do it as often as you should? The fact is it's on your list. You're committed to doing something about it. As you'd say to a friend in your position, you must start somewhere.

Instead of being critical of what you haven't done, be kind to yourself and recognize that tackling separation anxiety is tough. You deserve credit for even acknowledging your dog has separation anxiety. Many people don't even do that. And you're reading this book. That's taking action!

Focus on the Process, Not the Outcome

As James Clear puts in his book, *Atomic Habits*, winners and losers have the same goals. Every owner with a dog who has separation anxiety wants to get their dog to get past separation anxiety. That goal alone doesn't help us with motivation. Far more motivating is to look at the little wins—the tiny changes—and to celebrate those. Each step in the process that gets you closer to being able to leave your dog is a win.

The Importance of Realistic Expectations

What you do as an owner is the biggest factor in your dog's chances for overcoming separation anxiety. Your motivation and determination matter.

But there are downsides to being focused and committed: You're more impatient and have higher expectations. So when progress is slow (as it usually is) and you have setbacks (which you will), the more optimistic you are about training outcomes, the harder you'll take these blips.

I see it over and over: type A, focused, committed owners quit their training early. Not because they aren't capable, but because they had unrealistically high expectations of their puppy and the training.

Instead of expecting too much we need to reframe our thinking. In particular, it's essential to:

- Accept that you can't control this.

- Find a well of patience deeper than you've ever had.

- Expect slow progress at the start.

- Don't compare.

- Be an optimistic pessimist (or a pessimistic optimist).

- Find realism in the middle ground.

Accept that You Can't Control This

With separation anxiety training, you're changing the way your dog's brain is wired. While there are factors you can control (for example, how often you train, what type of training you do, and whether you use medication), you can't control your dog's neurochemistry. If you're someone who's used to taking charge and getting results, this will challenge you. But you have to accept that you don't get to control this.

Find a Well of Patience Deeper than You've Ever Had

Working with dogs requires patience. Working with fearful dogs even more so. You cannot dictate the rate of recovery. You just have to abandon notions such as "I need him to be over this by Christmas" or "I have to get him better by the time I go back to work." It's a cliche to say "it takes as long as it takes"—but it does. Imagining otherwise leads to disappointment. Sadly for us, our dogs aren't taking our schedule into account when they recover from fear.

Expect Slow Progress at the Start

I often hear grumbles that if it takes a month to get to one minute, how are you ever going to get to an hour? Separation anxiety training doesn't progress like that, though. You will spend a disproportionate amount of time on the early steps of training. You're building foundations. Have you ever watched a new building go up? If so you'll have noticed the early stages of clearing the ground and pouring the foundation take time. And once completed, you only see concrete. You can't see a new building. Then suddenly the structure seems to take shape. It seems like it becomes a building overnight.

I'm not saying you'll reach a point where training is so easy that you fly through it. It's just that plugging away at the start is valuable, foundational work. It's the sum of the tiny changes that leads to success.

Instead of obsessing over target times I ask my owner clients to take the pressure off themselves and their dogs. Instead of times we look at milestones: the first time you can take a shower in peace, or that lunch out with family that you haven't done in the longest time. You can see these milestones in the figure on the following page.

FREEDOM STEP	MILESTONES	FOCUS ON
Your dog gets upset when you go to the door. You're not ready to start departures.	**SHOWER IN PEACE** • You can open the door without your dog freaking out • Your dog might follow you less • Maybe you can take a shower in peace	• Use the door desensitization plan • Magic Mat to teach your puppy not to follow
Your dog can handle short training departures: minutes, not hours.	**STEPPING OUT** • Taking the garbage out • Getting something from the car • A quick chat with a neighbor	• Work on departures in line with your plans • Repeat, repeat! • Start to test out different scenarios
Your dog can cope with longer departures: 15 mins or so, but isn't always consistent.	**GRAB A COFFEE** • You can get away from the door (but not too far) • You might even be able to get a coffee (to bring home of course!)	• Rinse and repeat departure exercises • Work on unavoidable cues
Consistency around 30 mins or so. Some longer sessions but not predictably.	**BUY A FEW GROCERIES** • You dare to actually do something in the long absence, like picking up a few groceries or running a quick errand.	• Focus on building consistency, not just duration
Your dog is reliable at an hour or so. Your dog also seems to follow you less at home.	**CATCH UP WITH FRIENDS** • You can do a proper shop or quick catch up with friends • BUT you keep your camera on, ready to dash back • Starting to taste freedom	• Reward yourself with doing something away from the house (maybe 30 mins) • Double down on consistency
Your dog can now comfortably do 2 hours.	**DINNER, MOVIES, GYM, YOGA** • Fewer "formal" training sessions • Instead, you go to the gym, do stuff with the kids, have dinner with your partner • You're still watching and ready to dash back	• Do occasional formal training sessions • But also lots of cold departures • Mix it up
Your dog can be left on his own for as long as you need (3–4 hours).	**FREEDOM!** • Your dog has the occasional hiccup, but this doesn't undo his recovery • You finally stop feeling like a prisoner in your own home!	• Don't give up on the camera habit. It's a good habit to have • Be ready for regressions when life changes happen

Don't Compare

"Comparison is the killer of joy," as the saying goes. Never is this more true than with separation anxiety training. When you have a bad day, it can seem like everyone else is acing it. When you feel stuck on two minutes, you'll feel that the only posts you see are owners celebrating two hours.

Comparing will only make you feel worse about where you are right now. And those successes? They started out on seconds and felt stuck at times. Don't compare your beginning to someone else's end.

Be an Optimistic Pessimist (or a Pessimistic Optimist)

Optimists start things and quit when their hopes are dashed. The downside of being a pessimist is that sometimes you never get started in the first place.

With separation anxiety a middle ground is best. In other words, go into the process with hope but know that it might not work for your dog or that if it does it will take way longer than you hope. Let's be honest: Getting a puppy over separation anxiety could take months. It might be less, but it could be a drawn-out process.

And while we say we know that, and are okay with that, we're really not. We need this to be over. We need to get our lives back—now. But you'll be more successful if you forget the time line and just take it day-by-day. Remember what you can control, and what you can't.

Also call on the pessimistic side of you, which asks, "What will I do if my puppy doesn't get over this?" Reframe your thinking to

"Getting my puppy over this isn't the be all and end all."

It might feel like it, but the more you define your life by having a dog you can leave, the more pressure you'll feel with training. And this training doesn't work when either you or your dog are under pressure. We always weigh the impact of future negative events higher than we do when we review past negative events.

> ❚❚ Go into the training process with hope but know that it might not work, or that if it does it will take longer than you hope.

Think about a time when you worried about something beforehand, but when you look back on it, it wasn't that bad. Equally, we put more weight on positive outcomes when we look ahead than we do when we look back. That's why a) it can seem like our world will fall apart if we can't get our puppy over separation anxiety and b) we think that our problems will be solved when we do.

In truth, if you can't get your puppy over this you will survive. It will be tough, but you will be okay. On the other hand, if you do get your puppy over this, life will be so much better, but it isn't the only key to happiness.

Find Realism in the Middle Ground

If your feelings about the training are up and down, here are two exercises you can use when you feel the pressure of training not going to plan:

1. Take a tip from cognitive behavioral therapy (CBT). Do a "shades of gray" exercise. When you have an extreme negative thought, write down the exact opposite.

Then think of something in the middle that is actually anchored in reality.

Here's an example:

"This training is never going to work. I'm never going to be able to leave my puppy alone." (extreme negative)

"This training is amazing. I think he'll be fine in a couple of weeks." (polar opposite)

"Although things are slow, I can see how this will work. Some days he does really well with the training sessions." (realistic stance)

2. Instead of worrying about what might happen, focus on this very moment. Psychologists tell us that it's harder to be unhappy in the present moment. Right now, in this very moment, are you okay? Usually we are. But as soon as our minds wander to the future ("When will I ever be able to leave this puppy?") or the past ("Why didn't I do more research into separation anxiety before I got my puppy?"), we don't feel okay.

   Stay focused on the present. And that means staying focused on the process (that thing again!).

I say all this to you with love. Of course I want your puppy to be happy on his own. I want that both for you and your puppy. It's just that when you put too much weight on this outcome, training becomes harder and you are more likely to quit. Focus on the process.

When Training Falters

Even the most positive outlook and the best training habits won't steer you clear of bumps in the road. Setbacks are part and parcel of separation anxiety training. Everyone's training falters at some point. Knowing that, though, doesn't make it any easier when it happens to you. No matter how logically you think about it, and no matter how often you might tell yourself it will all be fine again, a setback can take the wind out of your sails.

The two main types of setbacks in separation anxiety training, and you'll likely experience both, are regressions and plateaus.

Before we talk about those, let's look at what a setback isn't. A setback is not:

- Having the occasional exercise in which your puppy does worse.

- Your puppy doing worse after a break or big change in routine.

Having the Occasional Exercise in which Your Puppy Does Worse

Variability in training is 100% normal. You will not have successful session after successful session. In fact, the more of a run you're on, the more likely it is that your next exercise will be a flop. Learning is never linear, especially when the learning involves overcoming a trauma.

There isn't a single dog who's overcome separation anxiety whose training progress doesn't look like a stock market chart: plenty of ups, but a good number of downs too. And just like the stock market, what matters is the overall trend. If you're training correctly, the chances are your overall trend is upward even if you have blips.

As we progress through training, we see that not only does the overall duration the puppy can handle go up, but their consistency does too.

These ups and downs in training aren't regressions. They are just normal variability.

Your Puppy Does Worse after a Break or Big Change in Routine

Anything can upset your training progress, but after a break from training or a significant change in your puppy's routine, you might almost expect him to struggle with his next exercise. I see this all the time in January when people have been off work, been traveling for the holidays, and had different people in their home. When they get back to training, it's almost as if the puppy has forgotten what they've learned.

When you train after a break expect your puppy to do worse. That way, anything else is a bonus.

Even though variability in progress is normal there's a chance that your puppy will regress—that is, he is way off target durations he was previously acing. Or your puppy may plateau, whereby his home-alone durations seem stuck around a certain time.

Regressions

Regressions are horrible to go through. In the depths of a regression, you think, "That's it. This is never going to work." It's almost unheard of for a dog to get over separation anxiety without a regression, and everyone who has ever been through a regression thought this, too.

It might not seem like it right now but, unless there has been a change in the puppy's world, there's a really good chance he'll get back to where he was.

You just need to drop back to a duration that your puppy is comfortable with and build from there. I know that will feel crushing. But you do need to go slow to go fast with separation anxiety training. Reducing duration isn't going backward. It's setting your puppy up for success.

What matters more than the time on the clock is you getting out of the door successfully. Every time you do that, you help your puppy's learning.

By reducing time to work back up, chances are your puppy will achieve the target duration (where he was before he regressed) more quickly than it took him to get there the first time.

Plateaus

A plateau is when the needle on your target duration just doesn't seem to shift. You go up a bit in one session, then down a bit for the next, then up again, and so on. Nothing dramatic—just a feeling of being stuck. Again, just like regressions, plateaus are normal, and they will happen.

Progression in learning is never a straight line. Yet we do tend to expect separation anxiety progression to be linear.

I liken separation training to track and field training. Each time your dog achieves a new target duration, they've set a new personal record. We expect them to do this day after day, and we are disappointed when they don't. We would never expect a high jumper or a sprinter to set a personal record every time they trained, though—and just because they don't achieve a personal record doesn't mean they aren't progressing.

If we stopped worrying quite so much about the clock, separation anxiety training would be much less stressful for us and for our dogs. Easier said than done, though.

Handling a Setback

If you are facing a setback, here's what to do:

1. Make sure there's no chance your dog could have had an over-threshold experience while he was at daycare or with the sitter, or when staying with friends and family.

2. Check that you haven't been training too much or too little. The sweet spot is about five or so exercises a week.

3. Re-watch the video of your training sessions (make sure you are recording) to see if there are any signs of anxiety you might be missing.

4. Think about what else might be going on in your dog's world. Has anything changed? Could there be something going on outside? Is there anything medical going on?

5. Review the data you've collected and see if you can identify any emerging patterns.

Always go through this checklist in case you might be able to point to a reason for the setback, but know that a lot of times when setbacks happen you will be unable to identify a cause.

If you do spot something, you can adjust. If not, just stick with what you know: train at the dog's pace and ensure he never goes over threshold.

Why Setbacks Are So Frustrating

Rationally you know what you need to do. You need to go back a few steps and ask yourself, "What can my dog do now?" But doing that feels unbearable.

Instead, you try the same duration again. Nothing doing.

You rest for a day or two and try again. Same thing—pretty much a disaster. It feels like a futile game of snakes and ladders. It's as if you slid all the way down a slippery snake.

Starting over never feels good, even when we know it's the right thing to do. Have you ever worked all day on a document only to find you didn't save it?

You want to cry, scream, or throw the computer out of the window. You know you could re-create the work in about a quarter of the time it originally took, but you can't face doing that. It's not in our nature to be comfortable going back over old ground.

Remember, though: With setbacks, it's not really going back to square one or wasting effort. Every time you step out the door successfully your dog is learning that being alone is safe.

Whether you're out for five seconds or five hours, your dog gets another data point that tells him that you going out of the door doesn't result in the end of the world.

My training plans have plenty of short steps as well as longer ones, so that even if you don't achieve the target duration for the day, you still got lots of successful steps in. In fact, I encourage my clients to not just count duration but also the number of successful steps they have accumulated during training.

The number of successful steps is just as important to training progress as the pushes in duration.

Most people whose dogs have recovered from separation anxiety will tell you the bad days will happen—but that you don't lose all of your progress. When you look back on your progress, you'll see more good days than bad. And you'll see that the progress line trends upward.

On those days when your dog does regress, it's easy to forget all the progress you've made. This is why you should track training sessions. It's amazing how motivating it can be to look back at how far you've come.

When your next setback occurs, try not to think of it as a roadblock. Think of it more as a diversion with speed bumps. You'll get back on track, but you might have to take the more scenic route for a little while.

Owners who work with me in my Separation Anxiety Heroes membership use an app to chart their progress. To give you comfort that you are not alone when it comes to ups and downs, you can see images of owners sharing the progress charts taken from their apps on the resources page at berightbackthebook.com.

Proceeding with Caution

The absolute best way to minimize your chances of a setback is to set your puppy up for success with a training exercise that's within his capability, every single time. This means:

- Not increasing the target duration by too much from exercise to exercise.

- Reducing the time to a duration that you think your dog can achieve next time should he struggle in an exercise.

- Balancing both these decisions with the goal of training efficiently.

You want every exercise to be a success, so keep that principle front of mind when you decide what duration to aim for.

What if It's All Too Much? The Puppy Blues

No matter how positively you approach training or how well you handle setbacks, there will be times when it all feels too much.

I'm not going to sugar-coat what it is to own a puppy who has separation anxiety. You wouldn't be normal if you didn't, at least some of the time, feel at your wit's end.

Even owners of puppies who don't have separation anxiety will admit to times when they think, "This wasn't how I imagined it would be." Many people call this the *puppy blues*.

It's okay to feel this way, especially if you have a puppy you can't leave. For many of us, separation anxiety tests the bond with our puppy.

We know that it's not their fault they're like this, but we're worn down by feeling like prisoners in our own homes or by the constant complaints from neighbors. We love them more than the world, but we get pushed to our breaking point and our relationship with our puppy suffers.

Not How We Imagined it Would Be

When you commit to bringing a puppy into your home, you commit to being there for that puppy regardless of what happens. And you commit to that puppy for life.

I'm passionate about this.

However, I also believe that no one gets a puppy thinking that they might never be able to leave that puppy. Puppies and dogs deserve, and need, company, but that doesn't mean we get them thinking we'll have to be with them 24/7.

If we think that dogs should never be left, then we should also rethink the ethics of bringing domesticated dogs into our life.

When you find your puppy has separation anxiety and you learn that part of the training is not leaving them, that's a huge shock—and a huge departure from how you imagined puppy parenting would be.

The best puppy parents plan for care for their puppy when they are at work as well as consider who will look after their puppy when they go away. They may factor in the cost of daycare while they are at work.

But no one costs out weekday and weekend daycare, dog walking, evening pet sitting fees, and live-in vacation care costs for a puppy who can't be left. We plan for the dog we imagine we'll get. We don't plan for a condition that most people haven't ever encountered before.

We have a long history of idealizing our canine companions. From Lassie to Benji, from Marley to Beethoven, we love a good dog movie. And if you scroll through Instagram you could be forgiven for thinking that everyone has a perfect dog—except you.

No wonder we look at our own puppy and see flaws. And no wonder it's like a bomb being dropped on us when we first find out our puppy can't be alone.

The Dog Next Door

It's not just online dogs who appear flawless. Closer to home, everyone else's dogs can seem so well-behaved that you feel like you're the only one with a problem dog. Don't forget, though, that you don't always see the whole picture. You might see a dog who's superb off-leash at the park, but who is awful on-leash. Or you might see a dog who politely greets people in the street, but who bowls over people when they come into the house.

Of course, some dogs are easier than others. The dog who doesn't do anything his owners dislike is a rare beast. Dog ownership in the real world is nothing like it seems on Instagram.

What We Expect of Dogs

The high expectations we have of dog ownership can lead us to feel cursed when we discover it's our puppy who has separation anxiety. It's easy to think, "Why me?" Dogs who have separation anxiety don't stack up to the ideal. They often frustrate the heck out of us. We can't understand why they get so upset. After all, we're only going to the store/dinner/the gym/work. We always come back. So why do they freak out so?

When they do get upset, why do they need to bark incessantly, or pee in the house, or chew our favorite shoes, or try to eat their crate? It's so maddening, isn't it? If you've ever had these thoughts, you are not alone. We all have! It's normal.

When You Feel Burned Out

When the puppy blues hit and you feel burned out from having a puppy who can't be left for even a minute, here's what you should do: take a break and reframe your thinking.

Take a Break

Take a break from training—a day, a few days, whatever you need. Also take a break from thinking about training. Far better that you feel enthusiastic for training than you dread it and feel you have to force yourself to do it.

And take a break from thinking about your puppy's issues.

During your training break, just manage his separation anxiety as you already do with the help of friends, family, daycares, and so on. Meanwhile when you are with him, instead of doing separation anxiety training, do fun things. Focus on all the things you love about your puppy. Take part in activities that bring out the best in him.

Reframe Your Thinking

Having a puppy who has separation anxiety can leave you feeling overwhelmed, judged, stressed out, tired, and defeated.

It might seem like the world has conspired against you. Your puppy, perfect in every other way, is breaking your heart with his fear of being left. And it might seem that there is nothing you can do about the way you feel. You can't help the way you feel. To a degree I agree with you here: It is a rotten condition, and you're only human if occasionally you think, "This isn't what I signed up for."

However, it's not true that we can't control our feelings. Our feelings are not dictated by events or circumstances. They are dictated by the thoughts we have about events or circumstances.

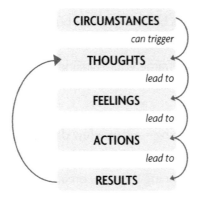

When your puppy can't handle being home alone, you feel hopeless. But it only feels hopeless because we *think* that there's no hope. In fact, when you step back you will see that there are options for helping your puppy be home alone.

What if instead of thinking, "There is nothing I can do," you think, "I'm going to investigate what I can do"—and then you think, "It looks like I can train my puppy to be home alone so I need to start that training."

Not having the perfect puppy might also make you feel like a failed owner. But you're not a failed owner. You just think you are.

You feel like a failure because you think that your puppy shouldn't jump up at people or shouldn't nip or shouldn't pull on his leash. You think other people will judge you.

What if, instead of thinking you're a failure, you think, "I can see that all puppies have issues. And sometimes people seem like they have perfect puppies, but in reality their puppy has issues too."

So the next time you beat yourself up or tell yourself this is hopeless, ask yourself, "Is that true? Or is that just the way I'm thinking about things?" If it's the latter, reframe those thoughts.

Dealing with Guilt

Another huge mindset challenge that we owners of dogs who have separation anxiety must face is dealing with the guilt that most of us carry. I've been there! I felt guilty for not spotting the signs early on with Percy. I beat myself up for doing all the wrong things when I did work out what was going on. And I felt continually guilty for the way my puppy's condition was affecting my family and friends.

Sometimes guilt is helpful, like when you know you need to do some exercise because you've been a couch potato all month.

Or when you haven't spoken to your mom for ages and you know she likes to hear from you. This type of guilt spurs us into taking the right action.

Other times, guilt is the projection of us breaking some invisible code or not meeting some impossibly high standards. Equally, we often find ourselves feeling guilty about situations we have absolutely no control over. This is when guilt becomes unhelpful.

After working with hundreds of owners over the years, I've identified a pattern in the types of guilt we separation anxiety owners feel, namely guilt over:

- Causing our dog's separation anxiety.

- Not doing enough.

- Making it worse.

- Medicating our puppy.

- Impacting our friends and family.

Let's look at each of those. Hopefully, I can convince you that you don't need to feel this way.

Causing Our Dog's Separation Anxiety

In "Can Puppies Really Get Separation Anxiety?" in Chapter 1 we covered that we can never know the exact reason an individual puppy develops separation anxiety. We do know what factors can contribute, including:

- What happened to the mother when she was carrying the litter and when the puppies were first born,

- The puppy's genetics,

- Bad experiences early in life, and

- Absence of socialization (lack of exposure
  to positive experiences early on).

As owners we might say that we could influence the third and fourth factors in the list. However, if no one tells us that it's not okay to leave a puppy who's in a panic to cry it out (bad early-life experience), and if we don't get guidance on home-alone training for our puppy (exposure to being left alone), how can it be our fault when we don't do these things?

For the most part, guilt that we caused our dog's separation anxiety stems from what others tell us, such as:

- "You're babying your puppy."

- "It's your own anxiety reflected in your puppy."

- "You need to just leave him to get over it."

Friends and family mean well. But I guarantee you if they are saying these things to you, they either have never had a dog who had separation anxiety or, if they did, they addressed it the old-fashioned way by letting their dog panic.

Once you have a puppy with separation anxiety, and once you know that means your puppy panics when you leave, you never say these things to other owners.

If you feel guilty that you caused your puppy's separation anxiety even though you know you didn't, you need to let it go. (This is true even if you think you did.) Worrying about what happened in the past isn't going to help your puppy. You need to focus on what you can control, and that's getting your puppy over his separation anxiety.

Not Doing Enough

You're over the hump of feeling bad about why your puppy has separation anxiety and you're focused on getting him over it. But even though you're taking action (including reading this book), you feel like you're not doing enough. You either don't train often enough or you're not doing "all the things" you read about that you think you need to do.

> ❚❚ The key is not to look at the mountain you think you have to climb, but rather to just focus on taking the next step. And then the next step.

Here's the thing, though: By reading this book you're already doing more than most people whose puppy has separation anxiety. If you're training, even just once a week, that's huge. And even if you're not training, but you've stopped leaving your dog, that's taking action too.

We can always do more. It's human nature to focus on the negative; which is why we ignore what we have done and focus on what we think we "should" do. But you're here, and you need to give yourself credit for that. The next time you beat yourself up about what more you could be doing, remember that with separation anxiety training most people don't ever do anything.

It's true that for a dog to get over separation anxiety you do have to put in a lot of work. However, the key is not to look at the mountain you think you have to climb, but rather to just focus on taking the next step. And then the next step. Climb to the top without looking to the top or you'll feel so overwhelmed you'll give up.

We humans never like to give ourselves a break, do we? Even after you start training you may still give yourself a hard time that you didn't start sooner. I wish someone had told you that as soon as your puppy comes home you should start home-alone training.

Most likely they didn't, though. And most likely you had no clue that your puppy would need to learn to be alone.

With the housetraining, the socializing, the puppy classes, and manners training, no wonder you didn't start home-alone training. That doesn't matter. What matters is that you're addressing it now. As the saying goes, the best time to plant a tree was 20 years ago. The second-best time is today.

It's the same with separation anxiety training. Sure, day one would have been the absolute best day to start. But today is a pretty good second-best day to start.

Making it Worse

Let's think about what we know about separation anxiety and what can make it worse. The number-one thing we have control of that can make a dog worse is leaving a puppy alone for longer than he can cope with. I don't think there's an owner out there who hasn't done this at least once. Of course, we feel guilty about it. No one wants to feel that their puppy was in a panic. However, most of us don't walk out of the door saying, "I'm going to teach that puppy a lesson and let him scream his heart out." We do it, or did it, because we:

1. Didn't know any better.

2. Were doing everything we could to manage absences, but then an emergency happened.

3. Thought he was being taken care of and didn't realize that puppy would be alone.

You often hear that ignorance is no defense. However, when

it comes to bringing up a puppy, I think it is. There is so much bad advice and misinformation out there that it's near impossible to get everything right.

You do your best. You buy the books, join the groups, and pay professionals. But the advice can be so conflicting that it's hard to know what to follow. That's why it can be so easy to slip up.

If you followed the advice to leave your puppy to cry, then you were acting in good faith. And you were paying people who should know better. Trainers should know better, but sadly many don't. Ignorance of the basics is inexcusable for a professional. In fact, it's criminal that people can take your money only to give out bad and potentially damaging advice.

Medicating Your Puppy

It's reasonable to feel this way because society as a whole stigmatizes the use of anxiety medications in people, so no wonder there's stigma about medicating your puppy. You might feel guilty because you feel this is unethical. Or maybe you feel guilty because of the side effects.

If putting your puppy on medication does violate your standards, ask yourself why you feel this way. Is this really your standard, or are you influenced by others? And why is this wrong? Is it just "something we don't do," or do you have a concrete reason for thinking that puppies shouldn't go on anxiety medication?

If your vet recommends anxiety medication for your puppy it's because these medications can help stave off a lifetime of chemical imbalance in the brain.

Anxiety medications are widely used for children alongside talk therapy. They help children overcome trauma, fear, anxiety, panic, and depression. Without them many children would be forced to carry issues with them into adulthood, when it becomes much harder to rewire the brain.

So if anxiety medications go against your principles, but you're prepared to go down that route for your puppy, then instead of feeling guilty you should feel proud of yourself. You're being selfless. You're putting your puppy's needs first.

Impacting Our Friends and Family

The family thing is tough. When you have a dog you can't leave, all sorts of tensions arise with friends and family. They judge you, give unsolicited advice (everyone's an expert!), and feel frustrated as you turn down invitation after invitation. You're caught between a need to do the right thing by your puppy and a sense of duty to your friends and family.

It's true that your friends and family miss you and feel let down. But they will cope, and it's not forever. You are not cutting ties with them. You're going to be out of circulation for a bit, that's all. You're just asking them for some patience and understanding in the meantime. To deal with this, prioritize who you spend time with, and invest your limited dog-sitting budget on getting a sitter for the most important events.

Then remember that most likely it's their disappointment at not seeing you that causes their frustration. They probably don't mean to guilt you.

If guilt is holding you back and making you feel even more miserable about your puppy's separation anxiety, ask yourself, "Am I right to feel this way?" If not, how could you think about things differently? Use this table to help you.

GUILT TYPE	IS THIS A REASONABLE AND RATIONAL THOUGHT?	WHAT STEPS CAN I TAKE TO FEEL DIFFERENTLY ABOUT THIS FROM NOW ON?
I feel guilty that I caused my dog's separation anxiety.	No, because even if you contributed in some way (unlikely) it's likely because no one gave you the correct advice.	Start training; suspend absences.
I feel guilty that I'm not doing enough.	No, because even by just reading these words you're taking action! This is more than most owners do.	Don't focus on all the things you could do. Instead set easy goals. Give yourself kudos every time you achieve a goal.
I feel guilty that I didn't start sooner.	Rational, maybe. Reasonable, possibly. Helpful, definitely not.	Look ahead, not back.
I feel guilty about medicating my puppy.	Yes and no. Yes, because there's so much stigma about anxiety medications. No, because evidence shows they can help your dog. Not rational but understandable.	Ignore the judgment or just don't tell anyone. Read up on the evidence of using anxiety medications for dogs. Keep reminding yourself that it's a welfare issue. Your puppy's brain needs help, and you are doing the right thing.
I feel guilty that my friends and family are suffering.	To a degree. Yes, their lives are impacted, but they will be fine.	Focus on quality, not quantity, and look for other ways to connect. Reassure them that you will be back.

Chapter Takeaways

- Mindset isn't the only factor in getting a dog over separation anxiety, but it is an important part.

- Finding and connecting with a community of people who understand will help you feel less isolated and more supported.

- Habits are far more effective than willpower when it comes to getting through difficult change.

- Regressions and plateaus are typical parts of training. What matters is how you respond to them.

- Setting realistic expectations, even if that means accepting that this will be a long process, is a more helpful process than just hoping for the best.

- Feeling guilty about your dog's condition doesn't help you or your puppy.

"

The problem is not that there are problems. The problem is expecting otherwise and thinking that having problems is a problem.

THEODORE RUBIN

CHAPTER 6

Dealing with Other Behavior Issues

While you might be focusing on getting your freedom back by doing separation anxiety training to get a puppy you can leave, you might also encounter other behavior problems that either interfere with your training or affect your quality of life so significantly that training is harder. This book isn't intended to be a compendium of behavior training for puppies. However, I do want to cover certain issues that I get asked about by puppy owners like you all the time, because they seem to happen often in puppies who struggle with alone time. In this chapter we look at:

- Problem barking,

- Nighttime anxiety,

- Attention-seeking,

- Chewing,

- Separation when out and about,

- Teaching confidence, and

- Puppies who don't love the car.

Problem Barking

You might be lucky and have a quiet puppy who hardly makes a peep. Or you might have a puppy who barks at everything (which is the case for many puppies!). If the latter, then you want to work on the barking, as it can interfere with home-alone training.

The most common types of barking are:

- **Watchdog or alarm barking,** which is where your puppy likes to alert you to outside noises he thinks you might need to know about,

- **Spooky barking**, which results from a puppy who is scared.

- **"Excuse me!" barking**, which your puppy might do when he wants something,

Let's take a look at each of those.

Watchdog or Alarm Barking

Train your puppy to do something he can't do at the same time as bark. Good choices are getting him to fetch a toy, getting out your Magic Mat (see "The Magic Mat Game" in Chapter 4) and asking him to stay on the mat for yummy snacks, and calling him away from wherever he's doing the barking.

You need to practice these without the doorbell or visitors first. Once he gets good at it, you can add those in. Don't worry if he doesn't get it the first time, every time.

See if you can get a friend or family member to pretend to be a visitor. This is an easy way to get lots of repetitions in.

Have another look at the Magic Mat Game. You can train your watchdog barker to go to his mat instead of barking.

Use a Fido Fine

Sometimes it can be helpful to let a dog know that he chose the wrong course of action. To do this, I use what I call "Fido Fines." Watchdog barking responds well to the signal a Fido Fine sends. This is not about scaring, hurting, or intimidating your dog. A Fido Fine is like taking an iPad away from a child who won't get dressed for school.

Here's how to use a Fido Fine. When your puppy barks at something outside, let him do a couple of barks, then ask your puppy to be quiet (say, "Quiet please"). Don't shout or yell; you're not trying to scare him into stopping. "Quiet please" is a warning cue that you'd like him to stop or else risk a fine. But keep your tone light and bright.

If he doesn't stop, "mark" the behavior you didn't want. Again keeping it light, say, "Oh! Too bad!" or "You lose." Now impose the Fido Fine. Either close the curtain to block the view (which is what your puppy wants access to) or remove him from the window, so that he loses access to whatever he was interested in.

No rough collar grabs and drags! Move your puppy calmly. You're not trying to scare him into stopping.

If he wasn't at the window when he barked, remove him from the room. Don't leave him. Stay with him without interacting. This is the one time when it is okay to ignore him! He's not upset so ignoring him won't stress him out. It is a nice penalty, though, and can help him realize that when he does the unwanted barking he loses stuff he values.

Your puppy will connect the behavior he was doing when you chirped, "Quiet please!" with the Fido Fine. Losing interaction with you, or to something interesting, is a big deal, so your puppy will start to choose not to bark. It might take a few tries, but keep at it and be consistent. Use a Fido Fine every time he doesn't follow the rules.

You can make this even more powerful by rewarding him if he stops after the "Quiet please" warning. Remember to have those treats handy!

Mask Outside Noises

If you have a puppy who barks at outside noises, one of the best things you can do is mask outside noise with noise inside your home. As much as it might seem annoying that you have to have noise inside when you'd really rather your puppy didn't bark in the first place, it's better for your nerves and for breaking your puppy's barking habit to not have noise that triggers him coming into the house.

There are two steps to take:

1.   **Sound-proof as much as possible**. This won't be easy, and there is a limit to how much you'll be able to do, but look for obvious points where sound comes into your home and see what you can do to minimize that.

     Windows are the worst culprits for noise leaking in, even

when closed. Curtains and blinds can help, but if you want to get fancy, consider window plugs. These are custom-made sound-proof boards cut to size to plug into your window frame. These might seem extreme, but when you have a dog who barks at everything, anything that makes for a quiet life is worth considering. Also think about entry doors. Use weather-protection strips to cover any gaps between the door and frame.

2. **Think about sounds inside your home that will mask noises from outside.** Consider radios, TVs, playlists on streaming services, white noise machines, and fans. Playlists are my go-to. I like the baby sleep playlists designed to mask noises in a baby's room.

Spooky Barking

With spooky barking, it's important to get at the underlying fear. You want to change how your puppy feels about whatever is scaring him.

To do this, whatever spooks your puppy must become associated with food. Whenever your puppy sees or hears something he's scared of, be ready with the best treat ever (chicken, beef, cheese, liver, burger—whatever he loves). You want him to start to associate the scary thing with the best food ever.

Let him see whatever is spooking him, then have a chicken or beef party. Don't get too close to the scary thing, though. You risk making him worse if you do. You can tell you've gotten too close when he either won't take a treat or chomps off your fingers when he does take it, or when you see signs of worry in his body language. If he's scared, put some distance between him and whatever's worrying him.

"Excuse Me!" Barking

Puppies don't just bark to alert us to things. They also bark when they want things: Our attention, some fresh air, a toy, another treat. They are especially prone to this type of barking when their exercise and enrichment needs aren't being met (see "Exercise and Enrichment" in Chapter 3).

❚❚ You need to be as determined as your puppy is.

So how do your deal with a pestering puppy? Well, dogs are brilliant behavioral economists. They excel at calculating how much effort to put into getting an outcome. If you ignore your pestering puppy, he learns he is wasting precious energy. He gives up and saves his effort for something with better odds. If your puppy could talk, we might hear him say, "This is dumb. I'm not getting anywhere!"

Letting your puppy get on with the unwanted behavior can sometimes be a good strategy. The fancy trainer language is *putting the behavior on extinction*. It works like this: Your puppy attempts the behavior and it doesn't work. He tries again. After seeing it doesn't work a few times, he gives up—eventually.

Although we can use extinction to our advantage, we must make sure our tactic doesn't backfire. If we're not careful, we can make the behavior stronger. If you give in to what I call the "Excuse me!" bark, puppies quickly learn barking works. And the more it works, the more they use it.

You need to be as determined as your puppy is. Stop rewarding unwanted barking with attention. Don't let him into the backyard if he's barking. Expect quiet before you let him out of the car at the park. Don't give in to barking at the dinner table.

Hold the line. If you crack, he gets rewarded—and he'll come back even more determined.

You may have been reinforcing his barking for a while by giving in. We've all been there! If so, expect his barking to get worse before it stops. You've changed the rules, and your puppy will be frustrated.

Remember, though, that letting a puppy bark it out is not what to do with a puppy who is anxious when home alone.

To help anticipate and pre-empt pestering puppy behavior, have a look at how much exercise and enrichment your puppy gets. Even if it seems adequate, persistent pestering can be a sign that he needs more stimulation. You may need to increase the fun and exercise he gets. Here are some suggestions:

- Take slow walks. These give your puppy an opportunity to catch up on the neighborhood smells. (Think of it as a "sniffari!")

- Play games with your puppy. Most dogs can learn to love games, even if they're not tug or fetch maniacs. Hide-and-seek and nose work are great for scent-driven dogs.

- Get him off-leash with other puppies (when he's old enough and fully vaccinated).

- Take him to safe puppy play classes.

- Ditch the boring bowl and let him work for his food. He'll love doing this!

- Scatter his kibble in the grass in the backyard, or on an area rug inside.

- Use his kibble for training treats. (Training tuckers pooches out.)

- Stock up on his favorite chew toys.

- Teach him to find a toy that you've hidden and then celebrate his find with tug-of-war or fetch.

Achieving Harmony

The key to a quiet life with a puppy who doesn't bark all the time is to work out which type of barking you're dealing with, and then to tackle that barking using the suggestions here.

Some dogs are just more vocal than others. Achieving a perfectly quiet dog is almost impossible. And even if you could achieve it, the training required would become a full-time job.

Unless your puppy barking is getting you into trouble with neighbors, creating chaos on Zoom calls (though try the cool noise-canceling app called "Krisp" if this is your house), or causing arguments with your other half, then sometimes acceptance that barking is just your puppy's way of expressing himself is the best course of action.

Remember that anxious barking—the type a puppy does when he's panicking at home—can only be stopped once you stop the fear.

Nighttime Anxiety

Nighttime anxiety happens when your puppy cannot cope with sleeping alone. This isn't a puppy who just thinks your bed is the comfiest spot in the house (so why on earth would they want to sleep elsewhere?), it's a puppy who gets anxious when not with you at night.

Why Dogs Like to Sleep on Our Beds

Given the choice, most puppies would prefer to sleep on a bed with their human. You may have read that when a dog sleeps on your bed he's asserting his dominance or leadership over you. This isn't true.

There's no evidence that dogs are in any way trying to be our leader. The alpha myth has long been debunked. The real reason that dogs like to sleep on our beds is that beds are comfortable. Dogs are social sleepers, so a comfy spot where everyone is sleeping is the natural spot for dogs to head to at bedtime.

When your puppy first comes home, he will have been sleeping socially every night of his life. For the most part that won't have been with a human, but it will have been with a bunch of other warm bodies. If you've ever observed a litter of puppies sleeping together, all piled up in a cozy heap, it's little surprise that your puppy wants to do the same with you when he comes home.

It's not uncommon for puppies to be unsettled at night especially when they first come home with you. That's why I like to approach resolving nighttime issues in stages.

Stage 1: Preventing Nighttime Issues

Decide where you want your puppy to sleep long-term. If you are happy for him to sleep on your bed, then you need read no further. If you don't want him to sleep on your bed, decide whether you're okay with him in your room or whether you want him out of the room entirely.

If you decide your puppy needs to sleep separately, then on

the first night have him sleep with you but in a spot other than your bedroom. This could be a sofa or a spare bed. True, spending the night on the sofa is no fun, but neither is listening to a crying puppy all night.

On the second night, sleep with your puppy in the room but not with you.

Then over a series of nights move your puppy away.

Stage 2: Resolving Nighttime Issues

If you followed the steps in Stage 1 but your puppy's nighttime issues aren't resolved, then move onto the following steps.

Teach Your Puppy He Can Sleep with You Out-of-Sight

While I don't recommend out-of-sight training for every puppy, it can be helpful for a puppy who can't settle on his own at night. You want to teach your puppy that he can handle being at home with you in another part of the house.

Use the Magic Mat training and do it in the spot you are going to designate as your puppy's sleep zone. Start by working on Magic Mat during the day. (See "The Magic Mat Game" in Chapter 4.)

Gradually increase the time you are out-of-sight. Your goal is to be able to go upstairs and spend 30 minutes in your bedroom with your puppy staying wherever you want him to sleep. Whenever your puppy breaks the stay and comes to find you, take him back to the mat. It's important that you do this consistently. He needs to learn that a) he's okay on his own on the mat and b) following you upstairs doesn't mean he gets to stay upstairs.

Repeat the steps in the Magic Mat training, but do so in the evening.

Then do Magic Mat training at bedtime. In order to make this as easy for you as possible, I recommend heading to bed an hour earlier. This might be hard, given your busy schedule. But far better to do this training and still have your full complement of sleep than be sleep-deprived.

Don't jump from one hour out-of-sight in the evening to a full night. Start with one hour per night. Then two.

Be Consistent

Depending on whether your puppy starts out sleeping separately but comes to your room at night or has been sleeping on your bed for some time, you'll choose a different course of action.

For Puppies Who Come to Your Room

Once you know that your puppy can sleep on his own elsewhere—because he's demonstrated as much with the foundational out-of-sight training you did—now is the time to tough it out. If he cries, go to him, but do not let him come into the room.

It's critical that if your dog wakes up, you don't let him scream, whine, or cry it out. Equally, if he does vocalize, don't just let him onto your bed. Go to him, but—just as you do with children—try to resettle him there rather than bringing him into your room. When you first start this process, you can resettle him by sitting next to his bed. Gradually move away so that you might settle him while sitting on a chair next to his bed, sitting further away from him and then standing.

You might well experience the night of the 100 walks (or several nights of them!), but you do need to do this every time. Go to him, resettle him, go back to your bed, and repeat, repeat, repeat.

For Puppies Who Sleep in Your Room but Whom You Want to Sleep Elsewhere

Here you gradually move your puppy away from you. Your first phase might be to have him sleep on a bed on the floor beside you. Then you might move his bed closer to the door, then outside the door, and so on.

The same "night of the 100 walks" principle will apply here. If he wakes, tries to get onto your bed, or cries, settle him in his bed. No matter what, he is not going to sleep on your bed. If you've completed the out-of-sight foundations, then you know he's okay sleeping separately from you. You know that he'd just prefer to sleep with you.

Don't risk it by letting him cry it out. You must go to him but always settle him on his bed.

Nighttime training isn't easy. In the short term you're going to have some sleep deprivation and disrupted nights, but if you're consistent and stick to your guns you can teach your puppy to sleep in his own space.

Attention-Seeking

You will find your puppy doing things that drive you bonkers. "It's like he knows how to push my buttons," you'll think of your little angel. Puppies are learning all the time and are constantly trying to make sense of their world. They learn what's safe and what's dangerous, and they learn what makes the world a better place for them.

One thing in particular that makes them happy is access to you.

And that's why your puppy might quickly develop behavior that aims to get your attention. Sometimes this is welcome, but often the behavior happens when we're cooking, trying to work, or on a Zoom call. Here's what you can do to tackle this problem:

- Be proactive first

- React to the problem as required

- Be consistent and patient

- Recognize the difference between wanting and needing attention

Be Proactive First

- Give your puppy plenty of attention, but decide the schedule for this. Having a schedule sets boundaries for both of you. A schedule doesn't mean spending most of your time ignoring him. (You didn't get a puppy to ignore him!) It just sets limits to interaction.

- When you interact, use a visual cue that says, "We get to play and cuddle now" so that when the cue isn't there he knows it isn't his time. If you work from home, you have an obvious and natural one: laptop open vs. laptop closed. You could also get a specific toy out. Even if you don't play with that toy, it's a sign that it's his time.

- Reward your puppy when he's quiet and isn't seeking attention. Don't make a huge fuss, though, as he'll see that as a sign that it's time to interact. An ear ruffle, praise, or a small treat will work here.

- The best time to deal with attention-seeking behavior is before it starts!

React to the Problem as Required

If your puppy has started to demand your attention in a persistent and pestering way, still follow the strategies listed in the prior section. However, you also want to deal with the behavior as presented.

- When he pesters you (provided he's had his scheduled time, and provided you know that it is just pestering and that he's okay), ignore him. Don't say anything or interact in any way. He is pestering to get you to interact. If you interact in any way, you reinforce that behavior.

- If he backs off and settles, reward him for that (keep the reward low key!). In case you're wondering whether this is teaching him a chain of behaviors (i.e., pester and back off to get rewarded), it won't. He wants your attention, and if he learns that the quickest way to get that is to settle on his own, he'll cut out the pestering.

- Use the training exercise I call Magic Mat (see "The Magic Mat Game" in Chapter 4) to teach him that being away from you is rewarding. When you have something important starting, get the Magic Mat out as a cue to him to go settle there. As a puppy he will need to be occupied, so add in a puzzle feeder to make him stay on his mat for longer.

- If crate training is going well, pop him gently in his crate if his pestering is too much. It's amazing how putting a puppy who loves their crate in there can activate an "off" switch. It's a bit like putting a toddler down for an afternoon nap.

- Teach him behaviors that require patience. Again, the Magic Mat will help you here, but you can also ask him to wait at doors and sit for greeting visitors.

Be Consistent and Patient

Above all, keep at this. You won't change his attention seeking in one day. You'll need to dig in. And know that he might get more pester-y before he gets better.

Get the whole family on board. Everyone has to do the same thing for this to work.

Recognize the Difference between Wanting and Needing Attention

Make sure you understand the difference between his *wanting* attention and *needing* it. If he's scared and panicky, his attention-seeking will be based on needing to be comforted. It's like the difference between a toddler who wakes with a nightmare and one who learns that if they ask you for a glass of water at 2 a.m. you'll get up and interact with them.

Chewing

It can seem like those little needle teeth are out to get everything: your hands, clothes, you brand-new heels, the TV remote, your scatter cushions, the dining table legs. You name it, your puppy seems to want to chew it. That is perfectly normal. Puppies chew because chewing is fun. They may also chew because chewing soothes their sore, teething gums.

Whatever the reason, puppies love to chew. They chew for fun in the same way that human toddlers like to play with building blocks or stuffed toys.

Sometimes puppies, and dogs, chew when they are anxious. If

you only see your puppy chew when you're gone, then this chewing might be how the puppy deals with the stress of being left alone. However, if your puppy chews at other times too, it's most likely the puppy having a good time. Puppies are skilled at learning the difference between chew objects that they are allowed to chew and forbidden ones. Part of growing into an adult dog is learning what's okay to chew and what's not.

It may take a while, and in the meantime you need to protect yourself and your belongings, but as puppies mature they learn what they are allowed to chew and what they may not.

Here's how you teach them:

1. Give your puppy items that you are happy for him to chew. Find out what type of textures and materials your puppy likes to chew: soft or hard, crinkly or fluffy? Does he really like to dissect rather than chew? Would he prefer an edible chew, or does he like to chew on objects?

2. Give puppies free access to these toys (supervised).

3. When your puppy bites or chews on items he shouldn't, just swap out the illegal item for an approved one. Do this every single time. Consistency is key. And make sure you do it without fuss and definitely no scolding.

4. If your puppy prefers to chew on you rather than anything else, you can use a quick penalty when those needle teeth are jabbed into your skin. As soon as his teeth make contact with your skin, step out of the room briefly. By losing access to you, you've just given him a penalty for teeth on skin.

By employing all these four steps you'll help your puppy learn new chew rules.

When you're trying to stop your puppy chewing things he shouldn't, make sure he has a plentiful supply of legal chews. Here are some ideas.

For Puppies Who Prefer Edibles

- Bully sticks (Always get size-appropriate ones and be ready to take the end piece away from him, swapping with a yummy treat as you do so, to help prevent any guarding tendencies.)

- Stuffed food toys

- Vegetables such as carrots or sweet potatoes, sliced into puppy-sized pieces

Avoid raw hide. It's a choke hazard for puppies and dogs and not great for their tummies, either.

For Puppies Who Like to Dissect and Shred

- Paper balls in a cardboard box

- Soft toys (Be vigilant about making sure your puppy doesn't get to the squeaky if there is one.)

- Rubber puzzle balls filled with rags or paper

For Puppies Who Like to Gnaw on Different Surfaces

- Purpose-made puppy chew toys

- Soft toys made from different fabrics

- Puppy-specific rubber toys

Part of growing into an adult dog is learning what's okay to chew and what's not.

Separation When Out and About

Not only do some puppies get upset when left home alone, but a good number also struggle with separations when out and about. You might have noticed your puppy cry when you go into a shop while another family member waits outside, or perhaps your puppy struggles with separations when you are on walks or when you're in a restaurant or on the patio.

This behavior is actually common, and many dogs who are fine when left home alone suffer from this.

You can work on this problem using the plan outlined in this section. But before you do that, consider how big an issue this is for you. For most owners, while this problem is frustrating, even upsetting, it doesn't happen often and doesn't affect quality of life the way home-alone anxiety does. Therefore, it isn't always worth the investment in the time that it takes to get a puppy over this.

As much as it's disappointing not to be able to take your puppy everywhere—especially when your puppy has separation anxiety and you're trying to manage absences—this behavior issue is a much easier one to manage than it is to train.

If I haven't persuaded you otherwise, here's the training plan to use:

What You'll Need

- Lots of delicious treats,

- A helper,

- A location you want to prioritize, and

- Your puppy's leash. (The plan is done with your dog leashed.)

GOAL #1

Getting Your Puppy Comfortable with You Being 100 Feet (30 Meters) away from Him, while a Helper Holds His Leash

SUCCESS TIPS:
- *Repeat each step until your puppy starts to look like he's anticipating a treat when you step away.*
- *You need to pause for 30–60 seconds between each repetition.*

STEP	WHAT YOU DO	WHAT YOUR HELPER DOES
1.	Move arm's length away from your helper for a count of 2, step back.	Your helper happy talks to your puppy and gives him a flow of amazing treats. The helper stops the treats as soon as you take the step back.
2.	Walk 6 feet (2 meters) away from your helper.	Wait until you take your first step, then your helper starts the happy talk and a flow of amazing treats. The helper stops the treats as soon as you turn to come back toward them.
3.	Walk 13 feet (4 meters) away from your helper.	Wait until you are 6 feet (2 meters) away, then your helper starts the happy talk and a flow of amazing treats. The helper stops the treats as soon as you turn to come back toward them.
4.	Walk 25 feet (8 meters) away from your helper.	Wait until you are 13 feet (4 meters) away, then your helper starts the happy talk and a flow of amazing treats. The helper stops the treats as soon as you turn to come back toward them.
5.	Walk 50 feet (15 meters) away from your helper.	Wait until you are 25 feet (8 meters) away, then your helper starts the happy talk and a flow of amazing treats. The helper stops the treats as soon as you turn to come back toward them.
6.	Walk 75 feet (20 meters) away from your helper.	Wait until you are 50 feet (15 meters) away, then your helper starts the happy talk and a flow of amazing treats. The helper stops the treats as soon as you turn to come back toward them.
7.	Walk 100 feet (30 meters) away from your helper.	Wait until you are 75 feet (20 meters) away, then your helper starts the happy talk and a flow of amazing treats. The helper stops the treats as soon as you turn to come back toward them.

GOAL #2

Getting Your Puppy Comfortable with You Being out of Sight, while a Helper Holds the Leash outside a Shop for 5 Minutes

SUCCESS TIPS:
- *Repeat each step until your puppy starts to look like he's anticipating a treat when you step away.*
- *You need to pause for 30–60 seconds between each repetition.*

STEP	WHAT YOU DO	WHAT YOUR HELPER DOES
1.	Stand next to the entrance to the store with your helper next to you holding your puppy's leash. Step inside the store and immediately back out.	Wait until you take your first step, then your helper starts the happy talk and a flow of amazing treats. The helper stops the treats as soon as you can be seen coming out of the store.
2.	Step inside the store and walk five steps. Turn around and exit.	Wait until you take your first step, then your helper starts the happy talk and a flow of amazing treats. The helper stops the treats as soon as you can be seen coming out of the store.
3.	Step inside the store and walk 10 steps.	Wait until you take your first step, then your helper starts the happy talk and a flow of amazing treats. The helper stops the treats as soon as you can be seen coming out of the store.
4.	Step inside the store and walk 20 steps.	Wait until you take your first step, then your helper starts the happy talk and a flow of amazing treats. The helper stops the treats as soon as you can be seen coming out of the store.
5.	Step inside the store and stay inside the door for 1 minute.	Wait until you take your first step, then your helper starts the happy talk and a flow of amazing treats. The helper stops the treats as soon as you can be seen coming out of the store.
6.	Step inside the store and stay inside the door for 1 1/2 minutes.	Wait until you take your first step, then your helper starts the happy talk and a flow of amazing treats. The helper stops the treats as soon as you can be seen coming out of the store.
7.	Step inside the store and stay inside the door for 2 minutes.	Wait until you take your first step, then your helper starts the happy talk and a flow of amazing treats. The helper stops the treats as soon as you can be seen coming out of the store.

STEP	WHAT YOU DO	WHAT YOUR HELPER DOES
8.	Step inside the store and stay inside the door for 3 minutes.	Wait until you take your first step, then your helper starts the happy talk and a flow of amazing treats. The helper stops the treats as soon as you can be seen coming out of the store.
9.	Step inside the store and stay inside the door for 4 minutes.	Wait until you take your first step, then your helper starts the happy talk and a flow of amazing treats. The helper stops the treats as soon as you can be seen coming out of the store.
10.	Step inside the store and stay inside the door for 5 minutes.	Wait until you take your first step, then your helper starts the happy talk and a flow of amazing treats. The helper stops the treats as soon as you can be seen coming out of the store.

Once you can comfortably stay inside the store for five minutes, extend the time as required.

If at any stage of this plan your puppy seems upset, return to the previous step and repeat that until your puppy shows happy anticipation again.

Teaching Confidence

Confidence in dogs is not a personality trait. It's context-specific. That big, bouncy, forward dog who seems confident might freak at paper bags blowing in the wind.

Why is that? Well, when we think of confident people, we're really thinking of people with high self-esteem. We use the word *confident* to describe people who seem to be comfortable in a wide range of scenarios, especially social settings. But this is just self-esteem. Those people might have scenarios in which they feel uncomfortable. Confidence is context-specific for people, too.

Can We Boost Confidence in Puppies?

Yes. But just as with people, to teach a puppy confidence we need to teach them confidence in a context. If you want your puppy to be more comfortable around people with hats, you need to teach him confidence around people with hats.

Consider this example: Learning how to play tennis won't make you more confident as a public speaker. To be more confident speaking in public, you might need to take presentation courses, work with a voice coach, or do some amateur dramatics.

As much as puzzle feeders or foraging for his food will make your dog feel happy, it won't help him feel more confident with, say, vet visits. The only way to teach home-alone confidence is with home-alone training.

Your puppy needs to learn confidence—and there are ways you can help him.

1. Socialization

Socialization (which we cover in Chapter 3) is technically a process that involves young puppies, typically up to 12–14 weeks old. The process of socialization, in which we gently expose them to new experiences and create positive associations with those new experiences, helps puppies be confident with whatever life has to throw at them as they mature.

However, while the socialization window closes as early as 12 weeks, that doesn't mean we can't continue to help our older puppies and adult dogs to have positive experiences.

To help a puppy or adult dog feel confident around different things in his life, we should always stick to these rules:

- Never push a dog into a situation in which he is uncomfortable. (You should be able to tell from body language or whether the dog willingly approaches a person or object.)

- Just as you do with desensitization training for separation anxiety, see if you can break new experiences into small, non-threatening steps.

- Aim to pair new or different experiences with something amazing (like chicken or cheese).

- When a dog seems uncomfortable, let him retreat. Always let him tell you whether he is okay.

These rules are especially important for helping a shutdown dog with general anxiety.

2. Choice-Based Training

Rewards training is the ultimate in giving dogs choice. They can choose not to do the behavior you've asked for. They can tell you when you've set the bar too high and it's stressing them. And they can choose to walk away when your training gets sloppy or you don't pay them fair wages for the work you've asked them to do.

Rewards-based training rewards dogs for getting the right answer. Dogs who are trained using this method want to do what you ask because:

- Something amazing might happen if they get the right answers, and

- Nothing bad will happen if they get the wrong answer.

As a result, they develop the confidence to try (because getting it wrong doesn't result in an unpleasant outcome) and they become more resilient. Getting it wrong is no big deal, and when you train well, there should be way more right answers. They start to learn that getting it wrong actually means there's a good chance they'll get the next one right. Hence, they aren't deterred by getting it wrong.

At every step they get to choose what happens next. This decision-making boosts their problem-solving and the result is a dog who seems happy and comfortable.

It's wonderful to see dogs who have been reward-trained react to a new training session. They respond with giddy excitement and anticipation!

3. Home-Alone Training

Puppies who are confident in every other aspect can still get scared when home alone. That's why we have to use the training in this book to teach how to be confident when left. We can do all the confidence-boosting we like, but we must do context-specific home-alone training so that your puppy learns to be okay on his own.

Puppies Who Don't Love the Car

While some puppies relish trips in the car, some puppies struggle with being in the car. To help your puppy be one of the ones who's fine on car journeys, here's what you can do. When you first bring your puppy home, make his first trip in the car spectacular. Have some high-value treats handy (chicken or liver treats are low-fat options) that first time he travels with you. Use high-value treats in the car the next few times you take him out. The treats together with trips to exciting places will help him love the car.

Some puppies don't travel well and actually get carsick, so if he starts to refuse the treats and you see him drooling or salivating, you might have a case of carsickness on your hands.

When puppies get carsick, they can start to dread car journeys, so if you suspect motion sickness, immediately chat with your vet. Your vet can prescribe medication to help your puppy feel less queasy. Make sure you do this, or you may end up with a puppy who dreads the car so much he will refuse to get in. Or, if and when he does get in, will shake, drool, and stress out.

Some puppies dislike the car even if they've been properly introduced to it and even if they've never had travel sickness. With these puppies, you need a plan to turn them from car haters to car lovers. The plan that follows will gradually desensitize your dog to the car while at the same time get him to associate it with amazing, yummy food, rather than scary things. This plan is for puppies who get anxious on car journeys, rather than puppies who whine with excitement in the car.

A few notes about this training:

- You're going to **need lots of amazing treats.** Why? Because we're going to change how your puppy feels about the car, by **making the car predict amazing things (i.e., food!).**

- Your puppy only **gets a treat after you start each step.** Don't give treats and then start the step. Do it the other way around!

- **Repeat** each step, and do it **as many times as it takes** for your puppy to look like he's loving that step.

- If your puppy looks scared by a step, stop. Then try an

easier step. Never force your puppy to do any step that makes him anxious.

- Follow this exact process at each step:

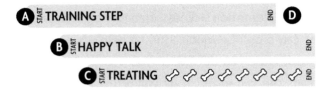

A. Start the step.

B. Start happy talk (or "Good boy" or "Well done," if you don't want to happy talk).

C. Reach into your treat pouch and start a very generous flow of treats.

D. Keep treating for a few seconds after you've finished the step

- Stick with each step of the following plan until your puppy seems to start anticipating treats when you do that step. (Yes, that means you could be walking to the car, opening and closing the door (Step 2) multiple times before moving on to Step 3 of getting the dog inside the car.

- Whenever you restart the plan, start at the step where you left off.

STEP	WHAT'S HAPPENING	WHAT YOU DO	SUCCESS TIPS
1.	Enter garage with your puppy (if your car is in the garage) and move next to car. If the car is parked outside, leash your puppy and take him with you to the car.	Do lots of happy, clappy "Who's a good dog?" talk as soon as your puppy sees the car. Then make it rain something amazing like cooked chicken, hot dogs, burgers, or anything your puppy finds irresistible!	Start to feed 2 seconds after your puppy has noticed car; continue feeding for 2 seconds after turning back on car. You can't be too generous!
2.	Open back passenger door; close door.	Do the happy talk and food again!	
3.	Open the back passenger door; pick your puppy up and place on back seat; close door for 30 seconds.	Same thing (more chicken!).	Feed your puppy 2 seconds after you put him on the back seat by dropping treats onto the back seat. (You might need to have the window open to do this.) Open the door just before your dog finishes.
4.	With back passenger door open, get your puppy to go onto back seat; close door for 60 seconds.	Yup, more chicken!	Feed your puppy 2 seconds after you put him on the back seat by dropping treats onto the back seat. (You might need to have the window open to do this.) Open the door just before your dog finishes.
5.	With your puppy on the back seat in car, close door; turn engine on.	Don't think I need to tell you!	Feed treats to your puppy on the back seat just after you sit down.
6.	Turn engine on; shift to drive; drive to end of driveway or 15 feet (5 meters).	Use happy talk but obviously don't treat until you stop. (This is where a remote feeder would be very handy.)	Feed treats to your puppy on the back seat as soon as you stop.
7.	Drive for a minute.	Happy talk plus delicious chew or other edible that will last more than a few seconds.	Use something that your puppy can chomp on while you drive. As soon as you stop, take it away so that your puppy thinks, "Oh, so I only get that when the car is moving."
8.	Drive to a green space or somewhere with lots to sniff, no more than three minutes away.	Happy talk, give your puppy a chew, then your dog comes out of the car on arrival for a good sniff.	The chew and the sniff are going to both help with your dog's association that cars = good stuff!

STEP	WHAT'S HAPPENING	WHAT YOU DO	SUCCESS TIPS
9.	Drive to the park.	Happy talk, something delicious to chew on, then let pup out at the park for huge after-car party! Repeat on way home.	Same thing: Getting to a fun place will reinforce how totally amazing the car is!
10.	Drive 5 minutes to somewhere less interesting.	Happy talk, something delicious to chew on, then let pup out at the park for huge after-car party! Repeat on way home.	You can now gradually start to build up from five minutes. Do different times and go on different types of roads.

Keep working through the plan until you have a puppy who's comfortable with car journeys.

Chapter Takeaways

🐾 Your puppy might not have any of these problem behaviors right now, but if he develops them you can use these plans even if he's an adolescent or adult dog.

🐾 Your training time is limited, so prioritize which problems you work on and which ones you just manage.

CONCLUSION

You might follow everything in this book to the letter and still be working on separation anxiety as your puppy grows into an adult dog. That's not because you did anything wrong or that the training doesn't work. It's because:

- For some puppies, no amount of prevention will stop them developing a fear of being alone.

- When it comes to changing emotions, there's no fixed timeline for recovery. It really does take as long as it takes.

- Puppies don't just grow out of it, so just because your puppy matures doesn't mean they will suddenly become okay with being alone.

If this is you and your puppy is now a grown dog who can't be left, don't give up. The training advice in this book still applies. You just need to keep doing more of the same.

This was never going to be an easy journey, but it could be an incredibly rewarding one. To this day, when I leave the house knowing that Percy will just be curled up when I'm gone, it feels amazing. I don't think that will ever lose its charm.

Countless owners like you thought their dog would never get over it. And while there can never be any guarantee with behavior change, separation anxiety training does work for many, many dogs.

There is hope for you and your puppy!

APPENDIX A

APPENDIX A

Sample Separation Anxiety Training Plans

Here are some sample **separation anxiety** training plans you can follow. Remember to always work at your dog's pace and under your dog's anxiety threshold.

Each of these training plans is based on the assessment of your dog's tolerance to alone time. Don't use these plans sequentially. Once you have successfully completed the initial plan based on your dog's baseline assessment, write out the next plan for your dog. See "Gradual Exposure Training Steps Explained" in Chapter 4 for a reminder on how to do this.

(You can find all of these PDF training plans online at www. berightbackthebook.com.)

Baseline Assessment: Less Than 10 Seconds

If your initial baseline assessment is less than 10 seconds, work on pre-departure cues or door desensitization training.

Baseline Assessment: 10 Seconds

Drop any avoidable pre-departure cues, step out of the door for the following durations, and return.

STEP 1	2 seconds	STEP 6	6 seconds
STEP 2	7 seconds	STEP 7	4 seconds
STEP 3	5 seconds	STEP 8	5 seconds
STEP 4	2 seconds	STEP 9	2 seconds
STEP 5	8 seconds	STEP 10	10 seconds

Baseline Assessment: 30 Seconds

Drop any avoidable pre-departure cues, step out of the door for the following durations, and return.

STEP 1	2 seconds	STEP 6	25 seconds
STEP 2	10 seconds	STEP 7	15 seconds
STEP 3	5 seconds	STEP 8	10 seconds
STEP 4	15 seconds	STEP 9	20 seconds
STEP 5	5 seconds	STEP 10	30 seconds

Baseline Assessment: 1 Minute

Drop any avoidable pre-departure cues, step out of the door for the following durations, and return.

STEP 1	10 seconds		STEP 6	25 seconds
STEP 2	5 seconds		STEP 7	15 seconds
STEP 3	10 seconds		STEP 8	35 seconds
STEP 4	2 seconds		STEP 9	20 seconds
STEP 5	20 seconds		STEP 10	1 minute

Baseline Assessment: 1 Minute, 30 Seconds

Drop any avoidable pre-departure cues, step out of the door for the following durations, and return.

STEP 1	5 seconds		STEP 5	15 seconds
STEP 2	15 seconds		STEP 6	20 seconds
STEP 3	30 seconds		STEP 7	10 seconds
STEP 4	5 seconds		STEP 8	1 min, 30 seconds

Baseline Assessment: 2 Minutes, 15 Seconds

Drop any avoidable pre-departure cues, step out of the door for the following durations, and return.

STEP 1	10 seconds		STEP 5	10 seconds
STEP 2	20 seconds		STEP 6	15 seconds
STEP 3	5 seconds		STEP 7	20 seconds
STEP 4	30 seconds		STEP 8	2 mins, 15 seconds

Baseline Assessment: 3 Minutes

Drop any avoidable pre-departure cues, step out of the door for the following durations, and return.

STEP 1	5 seconds	STEP 5	10 seconds
STEP 2	10 seconds	STEP 6	25 seconds
STEP 3	20 seconds	STEP 7	10 seconds
STEP 4	5 seconds	STEP 8	3 minutes

Baseline Assessment: 3 Minutes, 30 Seconds

Drop any avoidable pre-departure cues, step out of the door for the following durations, and return.

STEP 1	10 seconds	STEP 5	10 seconds
STEP 2	25 seconds	STEP 6	15 seconds
STEP 3	5 seconds	STEP 7	35 seconds
STEP 4	20 seconds	STEP 8	3 mins, 30 seconds

Baseline Assessment: 5 Minutes

Drop any avoidable pre-departure cues, step out of the door for the following durations, and return.

STEP 1	10 seconds	STEP 5	15 seconds
STEP 2	5 seconds	STEP 6	20 seconds
STEP 3	25 seconds	STEP 7	1 minute
STEP 4	10 seconds	STEP 8	5 minutes

Baseline Assessment: 7 Minutes

Drop any avoidable pre-departure cues, step out of the door for the following durations, and return.

STEP 1	10 seconds	STEP 5	15 seconds
STEP 2	5 seconds	STEP 6	20 seconds
STEP 3	1 minute	STEP 7	7 minutes
STEP 4	15 seconds		

Baseline Assessment: 10 Minutes

Drop any avoidable pre-departure cues, step out of the door for the following durations, and return.

STEP 1	5 seconds	STEP 4	20 seconds
STEP 2	15 seconds	STEP 5	1 minute
STEP 3	5 seconds	STEP 6	10 minutes

Baseline Assessment: 15 Minutes

Drop any avoidable pre-departure cues, step out of the door for the following durations, and return.

STEP 1	10 seconds	STEP 4	1 minute
STEP 2	25 seconds	STEP 5	20 seconds
STEP 3	5 seconds	STEP 6	15 minutes

Baseline Assessment: 20 Minutes

Drop any avoidable pre-departure cues, step out of the door for the following durations, and return.

STEP 1	25 seconds	STEP 3	5 seconds
STEP 2	1 minute	STEP 4	20 minutes

Baseline Assessment: 25 Minutes

Drop any avoidable pre-departure cues, step out of the door for the following durations, and return.

STEP 1	5 seconds	STEP 3	30 seconds
STEP 2	1 minute	STEP 4	25 minutes

Baseline Assessment: 30 Minutes

Drop any avoidable pre-departure cues, step out of the door for the following durations, and return.

STEP 1	10 seconds	STEP 3	45 seconds
STEP 2	30 seconds	STEP 4	30 minutes

APPENDIX B

Frequently Asked Questions from Owners about Training

've worked with hundreds of puppy parents over the years and I find that many of the same questions seem to be asked by many of you. Here are a few of the most common ones.

- He knows it's training, doesn't he?

- What if he does differently with different people or at different times?

- What if he follows me to the door during training?

- We have more than one dog. What do we do?

- What if both dogs have separation anxiety?

- Is it cheating if he's sleepy when I train?

- What if he falls asleep when we're training?

- Why is he so inconsistent with his training?

- What if I don't have time to train?

- Can I train him to be okay in another house?

Let's have a look at the answers to these.

Q| He knows it's training, doesn't he?

A| It might seem like your puppy can tell the difference between training absences and what you think of as "real life." But dogs' brains don't process the world in that way. Everything is real to them.

However, they definitely do understand *different*. This training that you do is leaving your puppy safely and with no more scary alone time. If your puppy has had bad experiences of being left in the past then he will start to think, "Oh, this one's different" when you start training. And that's a good thing! I want your puppy to think that the new way of being left is different. I want your puppy to think, "This is fine. I can handle this." That's why, when owners tell me that they're convinced that the puppy "knows he's training," I celebrate. It means the puppy is starting to learn that being alone is no longer scary.

Q| **What if he does differently with different people or at different times?**

A| First, we have the "what if" of different people, times, and context. Many dogs do differently depending on exactly what's going on in their world at that time.

As an example, some dogs train well in the evening but struggle in the morning. Some dogs do well on weekends but struggle during the week. Some dogs do better when Mom leaves versus when Dad leaves. Some dogs do better when it's cold out rather than when it's warm out. You need to think about all of these exceptions, and this is where that data you've tracked starts to come into play.

When you start to recognize that he does better in certain contexts than others, what can you do with that information? Prioritize.

If your dog does better with Mom than with Dad, but it doesn't really matter to you who leaves first and who leaves second, then put that to one side. But if, when you do the exercises, he does better in the evenings than during the day, and yet leaving in the day is the most important time for you, then you might want to work on that.

Use the following grid to help you. You can work on the easy, low-hanging fruit, or you can work on the tough ones because they're high priority. When you first start training, it's good to have some successes. I encourage people to work on the low-hanging fruit because it's motivating. You'll see more progress than if you tackle the big, difficult stuff in the top right of the grid.

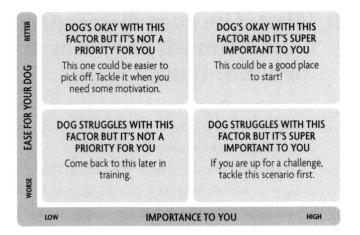

BETTER / **EASE FOR YOUR DOG** / **WORSE**	**DOG'S OKAY WITH THIS FACTOR BUT IT'S NOT A PRIORITY FOR YOU** This one could be easier to pick off. Tackle it when you need some motivation.	**DOG'S OKAY WITH THIS FACTOR AND IT'S SUPER IMPORTANT TO YOU** This could be a good place to start!
	DOG STRUGGLES WITH THIS FACTOR BUT IT'S NOT A PRIORITY FOR YOU Come back to this later in training.	**DOG STRUGGLES WITH THIS FACTOR BUT IT'S SUPER IMPORTANT TO YOU** If you are up for a challenge, tackle this scenario first.
	LOW **IMPORTANCE TO YOU** HIGH	

Q| What if he follows me to the door during training?

A| Doors are exciting things for dogs. If you think about it, a lot of fun stuff happens on the other side of the door: car rides, park outings, walks, exciting visitors arriving. No wonder dogs love to check out what's going on at the door. So no, following you to the door is not, on its own, a sign of anxiety.

If your puppy looks even slightly distressed, agitated, or panicky when you head to the door, that's different. In that case, your puppy following you is a sign of upset.

We also need to remember that no dog, even a non-anxious one, is happy when we leave. He might not panic, but he can be disappointed. After all, pretty much everything fun in their life happens when we're around or when we take them out.

I explain to owners that a natural progression with separation anxiety training is for a dog to go from anxious to disappointed. It's rare to see a dog go from anxious to delighted that we're leaving, so no wonder the following behavior can linger.

Q| We have more than one dog. What should we do?

A| Another dog may make no difference to your exercises whatsoever. Here are two scenarios in which it might:

1. Your anxious puppy is being triggered by the other dog's (non-anxious) barking at noises outside.

2. You try to do the exercises, and your second dog gets over-excited and sets off your anxious puppy.

If you're struggling with #1, then your best bet is to attempt to mask the outside noise with music or white noise. You can also train your non-anxious barker to be less reactive to outside noise. It's easier to put a halt to this type of barking when you're around, of course. When you're gone, there's no one to ask him to be quiet. You could well find that if you work on this reactive barking, it may well be less of an issue when you aren't there.

If #2 is your issue, then try crating the non-anxious dog or confining him to a different room while you train. If you think that your other dog makes your anxious puppy more comfortable, though, then involve that other dog in the training.

Lots of people worry that one day they're going to have to take their other dog to the vet or groomer, and how will their puppy be when their pal isn't there? But those are exceptional circumstances. Dog training takes a lot of effort, so it pays to train for the most common things first and then worry about the extreme exceptions.

Q| What if both dogs have separation anxiety?

A| This is not as uncommon as you might think. Some studies suggest that 20% of dogs have separation anxiety, so it's not improbable that two dogs in the same household might have separation anxiety. It's not that one dog caught it from the other dog, it's just that you got doubly unlucky.

If you have two dogs who have separation anxiety, your training will go at the pace of the slowest dog. Conduct the baseline assessment with both dogs present and note the time that the first dog gets anxious. As you progress through training, continue taking the lead from the dog who's finding training hardest.

Q| Is it cheating if he's sleepy when I train?

A| No, it's definitely not cheating if you train when your puppy is sleepy. In fact, I encourage you to do this. When we train a puppy to do anything, we always need to start with whatever is easiest. That's why we don't train a puppy to sit by starting in the dog park. We start our sit training at home because there's more chance of success. Once a puppy is nailing sitting on cue at home, we can try it outside.

We need to use the same principle for separation anxiety training. We start with whatever makes it easiest for your puppy and only progress to the tough stuff as we move through training. If your puppy does better when he's sleepy, train when he's sleepy.

One word of caution, though: Don't train when your puppy is fast asleep unless your puppy notices you going. If you try to sneak out, there's a chance he'll wake up and freak when he finds you're not around.

Q | What if he falls asleep when we're training?

A | Another side to sleepiness is a puppy who falls asleep during training. This is great! If your puppy is able to fall asleep while you're gone, he's clearly handling the departure really well. Don't be tempted, though, to stay out for as long as he's asleep. What we don't want is for him to wake up, wonder where you are, and then get upset. Stick to the time that you have in your training plan, and come back even if that means waking your puppy up.

Q | Why is he so inconsistent with his training?

A | If this is your puppy, you no doubt feel extremely frustrated. One day he can do 30 minutes, the next day he can barely do 30 seconds. Inconsistency is perfectly normal. We expect the progress to be a straight line, but it never is. What happens as we train is that, not only does the duration that he can achieve improve, but consistency improves. Everyone who has gotten their puppy over separation anxiety has experienced this. Just focus on getting in lots of successful training exercises and over time consistency will come.

Q| What if I don't have time to train?

A| There will be times when, despite your best intentions, you just feel like you don't have time to train. That's natural. After all, separation anxiety training isn't the most fun activity you and your dog could do together. I doubt anybody gets out of bed and says, "Woo hoo, separation anxiety training today!"

When you're not feeling motivated, plan some really short, easy sessions. Find just five minutes, and make a deal with yourself that you'll just do some Door Is a Bore exercises. As part of that deal, say that if you want to keep going after five minutes you will—but that if you want to stop at five minutes, that's absolutely okay. The momentum of getting going for five minutes might mean that you end up doing a full exercise.

This little trick of easy goal-setting is something that psychologists recommend we use whenever we feel stuck. For example, when I don't feel like going to the gym, I make a deal with myself that I'll get changed into my workout gear. Of course, once I've gotten off the sofa and changed, I decide I may as well go to the gym.

Give the sneaky little hack a try in other situations too.

Q| Can I train him to be okay in another house?

A| Remember we talked earlier about confidence being very context-specific, especially with dogs. They can learn to be confident in one situation but struggle in another context that doesn't seem any different to us. For example, your puppy might be frightened of men with hats but be fine with men without hats. That doesn't make sense to us, because what's so scary about a hat? But to a puppy a man with a hat might be a completely different beast than a man without.

And when it comes to home-alone confidence, I regret to say that it really doesn't translate from location to location. This means if you want your puppy to be happy in your own home and happy at, say, your parents' home, you'll need to train your puppy to be okay in both locations.

APPENDIX C

Handling Comments from Friends and Family

If you're struggling to know how to respond when friends and family challenge you about your puppy, here are some scripts to help you handle tricky conversations.

"Why can't you leave him? It's just normal puppy behavior. He'll soon quiet down if you let him get on with it."

"Yes, I can see why you would say that, and my trainer says even dog trainers used to think that too about puppies, but now we know they're not attention-seeking or getting mad at us for going out: They're having a panic attack."

"It's because you let him onto your sofa and you let him sleep in your bed."

"Dogs are social sleepers, and this puppy has just been plucked from all he's ever known. Lots of people do say these things cause separation anxiety. But no one knows for certain what brings it on. We do know how to fix it, though, and that's what I'm focused on."

"Surely you can leave him this once. It's only a movie/lunch/drink."

"I know it can seem silly that I can't leave him, but if I let him go over his fear threshold, he'll panic and have a setback. I risk losing all the progress we've made so far. If I stick to the plan, I'll be back in circulation soon enough."

"He doesn't still have separation anxiety, does he?"

"It probably seems like I've been working on this for ages, but what you might not know is that a puppy with separation anxiety has seriously messed-up brain chemistry. It's a deep emotional trauma on the same level as human PTSD, so can you see why it's not something that can be quickly fixed?"

"Puppies don't get separation anxiety."

"We definitely used to think that. But now know we know that puppies can, and do, get separation anxiety. Fear can be genetic, or it can be the result of early life experiences. I'm certain that my puppy was predisposed to separation anxiety even before he came home with me."

"Why don't you just crate him?"

"That would seem like the obvious thing to do, wouldn't it? I am working on getting my puppy comfortable with his crate, but it's a very slow process with a puppy who panics when left. You probably enjoy your home, but if it were on fire you'd run out of there in a panic. It's the same with puppies. They might love their crate sometimes, but when they are in a panic at being home alone, all they want to do is escape."

"It's your anxiety that's making him like this."

"You're right: I am anxious about my puppy. It's horrible to think of him out of his mind with panic. And I'm stressed about having to train him and to change my life so that he isn't left alone and scared.

"However, my anxiety results from his condition, not the other way around. There's no evidence that our anxiety causes separation anxiety. With human parents, yes, this can happen. But then, a part of that could be passing down anxious genes."

"He'll grow out of it."

"It's true that lots of puppies do fuss when separated from their owner and that it's just a passing phase. But what's going on with my puppy is more than that. Unless you've had a puppy like this, it probably seems silly that I can't leave him."

"All puppies cry when you leave them."

"Yes, you're right. It is really common for puppies to cry when they are separated from their owner. That's because being alone isn't natural for dogs. We get lucky with most puppies in that they do just learn how to cope with it. But unfortunately for me, my puppy is one of the 20% of dogs for whom being left isn't something they just get over."

"You can't put your puppy on anxiety medication. Who does that?"

"It's something that I've thought long and hard about. Like you, I used to think, 'Who does that?' because unfortunately there's a lot of stigma around anxiety medication generally—for dogs and people. However, the evidence shows that dogs who suffer from separation anxiety have issues with brain chemistry imbalances. All that anxiety medications do is help address that imbalance.

"And we know that puppies are not too young to be prescribed anxiety medication. The medication doesn't adversely impact brain development. Far from it: Medication helps them develop a brain that isn't permanently affected by fear. After all, children also benefit from anxiety medication, so brain age isn't an issue."

APPENDIX D

Success Stories

Now that you've finished the book you might be wondering what the future holds for you and your puppy. That's why in this section we talk about successes. I've included the stories of my clients as well as the clients of some of my Certified SA Pros.

Let's start with **my clients**.

- Signe and Bailey
- Carla and Ernie
- Helena and Reenie
- Louise and Treacle
- Peter, Lynn, and Archibald
- Jen and Gus
- Beth and Otis

MY CLIENTS
Signe and Bailey

Signe adopted Bailey, a Russian tsvetnaya bolonka, when Bailey was nine weeks old. Even from that very early age separation was a struggle for Bailey.

Signe was immediately overwhelmed with different advice on how to cope with it.

She was told to let Bailey cry it out, to not cuddle her as much, to ignore her upon return, give her activity toys when alone, not let her in the bed, natural remedies, plug-ins—"all the classics," as Signe calls them.

Before working with me, Signe did try gradual exposure training. But she admits that she was never truly on top of the signals Bailey sent during those exercises.

That said, Bailey did show some improvement. Sadly, though, Bailey got scared by a noise in the apartment building. This brought them back to zero. In fact, Bailey's anxiety was then even worse.

Signe then joined Separation Anxiety Heroes and started structured departure training using the Be Right Back App.

Signe and Bailey started to make solid progress. "Never have I seen her as relaxed as after doing SubThreshold training with her," says Signe.

Signe says that, as a result of the training, Bailey has grown so much more confident. She takes herself to different rooms to nap and even goes inside while Signe is in the garden.

Signe adds, "It's truly incredible to train her in a way where she always feels safe and comfortable—and I now have hope that we will have a normal life with Bailey. :)"

Bailey has now done up to three hours successfully and

relaxed on her tiny pillow. Signe advises, if you're starting this training, "Hang in there and trust that you're truly doing the very best possible for your separation anxiety pup."

MY CLIENTS
Carla and Ernie

Ernie is a handsome fawn whippet who lives with his human, Carla, in London. Ernie was a pandemic puppy, but not a spur-of-the-moment puppy. Carla had been planning on getting a puppy at some stage. The pandemic just brought that decision forward.

Almost from the outset, Carla noticed that Ernie became unsettled when she tried to leave. Carla was working from home during lockdown, so this didn't present a huge problem—at first. Like many people, Carla was pretty much at home 24/7 with her dog.

Nevertheless, she knew that Ernie's issue with her leaving wasn't something she could ignore. After all, at some point she did hope to be able to leave the house again.

Soon after discovering Ernie's issues, Carla came across my Be Right Back! Heroes Club. She learned about the training method you read about in this book. And she started training.

Ernie was a tricky one. The needle on his alone time really didn't move at all during those first weeks of training.

Carla, like many owners do, wondered whether this training would really work, and she doubted whether she would ever have the freedom to leave the house.

Not one to be defeated, though, Carla continued. As I say over and over, those tiny changes in the first few weeks, or even months, of training might not seem like much. In fact, they are often so tiny that we don't see them.

But they are foundational.

As Carla continued to put in the training effort, she started to see a change. She joined the one-minute club. Then moved onto the 10-minute club. In the Be Right Back! Heroes Club, we celebrate all those milestones.

We especially celebrate the one-hour milestones and were delighted for Ernie when he joined that club.

This makes it sounds like Carla and Ernie had a smooth progression. They most definitely didn't. As is normal for puppies who have separation anxiety, Ernie's recovery was up and down.

I've seen so many dogs recover from separation anxiety that I know this variability was normal. I just had to keep reminding Carla of this.

Bumps in the road for Ernie included when he seemed to be acing two hours but then suddenly would have a day when Carla could barely get out of the door.

Again, so normal! Dogs can be very inconsistent with their times as they go through the recovery process. With repeated training, not only does duration increase but so does consistency.

This is exactly what Carla discovered.

Brave little (now all grown-up Ernie) can now do well more than two hours, and has that consistency in the bag. He loves nothing more than to gaze out of the window and watch the world go by while Carla is out. Not anxious, not stressed—just chilling.

MY CLIENTS
Helena and Reenie

Reenie the cockapoo was eight weeks old when she went home with Helena. Helena sensed almost immediately that Reenie didn't like to be alone. Helena felt that it was as if Reenie was hardwired to develop separation anxiety.

Helena took Reenie to a doggy daycare at four months, but it didn't go well. Whenever the daycare staff were out of sight, Reenie would howl.

Hearing this prompted Helena to buy a camera. That's when she realized how much Reenie was struggling with alone time. Helen says it still breaks her heart to think back to those videos now. (I certainly recall that feeling.)

Like most owners when they discover their puppy can't be left, Helena tried a range of solutions: calming plug-ins, food distractions, relaxing music, talking through the camera, and covering Reenie's crate. None of these made a bit of difference.

She also tried the cry-it-out method that so many trainers still advise. Sadly, this resulted in Reenie worsening. She went from crying and howling to very heavy panting and getting increasingly panicky.

Helena knew she had to do something, or Reenie's condition would just deteriorate.

That's when she found my Facebook group and joined Separation Anxiety Heroes.

Helena started slowly with Reenie. She did the work. She stayed the course, and now Reenie can easily handle up to four solid hours!

Helena stuck with the training even when other people were

telling her it would never work, that it was such a drawn-out process, and that Reenie just had to get used to being left. In the end, like many of us do, she stopped telling friends and family about the training. Helena says, "My partner very much believed we should get her to cry it out at first. But now he sings my praises, as he can't believe the improvement!"

If you're just starting out, Helena has some advice for you: "The top tip I tell everyone now is go slow and steady! Do not push. Even if you think they can go longer still stick to small increments. It's a marathon, not a sprint."

MY CLIENTS
Louise and Treacle

Meet Treacle, the cutest golden cockapoo, who lives with his human, Louise.

Treacle always had issues with being left, and Louise's life was turned upside down by having to find ways not to leave him. Louise had a busy job and an active social life, neither of which are compatible with a dog who can't be left.

Louise knew how important it is for recovery not to leave a dog who has separation anxiety, so through complex arrangements involving daycare, dogwalkers, favors from friends, and meeting up in pubs that were dog-friendly, Louise was able to suspend absences.

She started the training on her own, and Treacle made some progress. But he would progress, and the slide back. Progress, and slide back again. It seemed to Louise that it was almost on a schedule. He'd move forward for three weeks then slide, and then progress.

Louise started to work with me and, sure enough, Treacle made good progress to start. He did, however, slide back too. I knew this was hard for Louise. I also knew, though, that we just needed to stick with the training, identify any triggers for the off weeks, and adjust if necessary.

It's always so much easier for me to hold my nerve because I've seen so many dogs and know that ups and downs happen.

One thing that Louise very cleverly identified was that Treacle, unlike many dogs, actually did better when he was upstairs in the bedroom.

Most dogs do better when they have free reign of the house. But for Treacle, this meant being able to hear noises from outside. These noises triggered him.

When Louise tried settling Treacle in her bedroom, it made such a difference. He was no longer troubled by the outside noise, and he soon became a little living rug on Louise's bedroom floor when she went out, handling the absences like a sleepy pro.

MY CLIENTS
Peter, Lynn, and Archibald

Archibald is a bouncy cavapoo who lives in the English countryside with Peter and Lynn. Peter and Lynn didn't immediately realize their new puppy had separation anxiety. He seemed fussy and got worked up when they left, but Peter and Lynn just assumed it was normal puppy stuff.

Occasionally, they came home to chewed shoe heels or nibbled corners on rugs, but they started to notice more and more scratch marks on the door where little Archibald had scraped away the paint.

They started to think that something wasn't right. Their suspicions were confirmed when their next-door neighbors had work done on their roof tiles. The roofers heard Archibald howling pretty much the whole time Peter and Lynn were out.

Naturally, Peter and Lynn immediately asked Dr. Google about "puppies who cry when left." That's when they first suspected Archibald might have separation anxiety.

They invested in pheromone plug-ins and an anxiety vest, as well as in a camera to watch Archibald. They were so upset by what they saw: Archibald cried nonstop when they left.

The vest and plug-ins made no difference, so they contacted a trainer. Sadly, the trainer told Peter and Lynn to crate Archibald, ignore him when he asked for affection, and immediately stop him sleeping on their bed.

Peter and Lynn followed this advice but it made no difference. Not only that, but they hated to ignore their gorgeous puppy, and it broke their hearts to hear him crying at night.

That's when they came across my previous book. The advice made much more sense to them, they said, and they loved the humane approach I advocate.

Lynn reached out to me, sensing that they might need extra help with the training. We started working together, and fluff-ball Archibald soon made wonderful slow and steady progress.

There were plenty of ups and downs, including a blip when Peter and Lynn moved to France. If moving home is tricky for a dog who has separation anxiety, moving countries is an even greater challenge!

But Archibald bounced back and continued his march toward home-alone happiness.

These days, Archibald is all grown up and handles absences

like a pro. Four hours of alone time is nothing to confident little Archibald.

MY CLIENTS
Jen and Gus

Jen and Gus are some of the most inspirational Be Right Back Heroes we've had in the club. Little Gus, the shih tzu Tibetan spaniel cross, is an old hand at acing alone time. But it wasn't always like that.

When Jen first joined the BRB Heroes Club, Jen couldn't even *think* about taking a shower without Gus losing it. Jen, despite the heartache of finding out her adorable puppy was a wreck who couldn't be alone, handled it all with humor and positivity. #gusjail became a familiar tag in our group.

As I've said to Jen subsequently, Gus was so bad that I did think, "Uh-oh, maybe he'll be one of the ones who doesn't get over this."

Silly me for underestimating these two!

Jen is one determined human—and Gus is one eager learner. How could I ever have thought that #teamgus wouldn't make it.

Jen trained and trained and trained. She found endless creative ways not to leave Gus alone. She even adopted a rescue dog, Molly, who had suspected separation anxiety. Jen says, "If I have to stay at home for one dog with separation anxiety, might as well take on another one!"

It turned out that Molly's anxiety at being left resolved quickly in her new home. (Note: Though Gus loved having Molly at home, she didn't fix his separation anxiety.)

Gus was progressing slowly but surely. However, one bump in the road that Jen kept facing was that every time she reintroduced departure cues, he freaked out.

What Jen did here was perfect: She kept training without the cues. Jen knew that Gus had to build home-alone confidence before he would be okay with the old cues.

It wasn't until about an hour until Jen was able to bring back those cues. When she did, Gus had become so comfortable with home-alone time that he didn't care one bit.

Perhaps my favorite ever post from Jen is the one where she shared pics from her first dog-free family lunch since discovering Gus's home-alone issues. The photos showed a gorgeous patio with to-die-for views—and not a pooch in sight.

It's not that Jen doesn't love lunches with Gus, it's just that she wanted to celebrate being able to choose whether to take him or leave him.

The lunch was made more special for Jen knowing that Gus was happily hanging out at home without a care in the world.

I loved getting this update from Jen, "Gus and Molly are still smashing it out of the park, and Gus just gets better and better. He's even given up his spot by the window when we're out now and goes off partying with Molly then sleeping with his back to the window. Little trooper has come such a long way!"

Way to go, #teamgus.

MY CLIENTS
Beth and Otis

Otis is a cuddly, happy bundle of fun. His big problem in life was that be hated it when his human, Beth, had to go out.

When I started working with Beth, she had tried different training methods and various remedies she'd found online. Nothing was working.

Not only was she struggling to find anything that would help Otis, but she was also dealing with comments from friends and family that she was being too soft, that she was coddling him, and that she just needed to let Otis get on with it.

Beth knew this wasn't the right approach, though, so she embarked on gently getting Otis used to alone time using the gradual exposure method we cover in this book.

Beth realized that, unlike all the other approaches she'd tried, this was different. Using the same method that we use to help humans over their phobias made total sense to Beth, whereas lots of other methods she'd tried hadn't.

She started to see slow and steady progress and saw that this could work.

But progress is slow with separation anxiety training, and it can also be sticky. This was tough on Beth, especially given the ongoing advice from people telling her she just needed to let Otis cry it out.

Beth knew this wasn't right, though and continued with gradual exposure.

There were plenty of days when it seemed like Otis had gone back to square one. When that happens, it makes you want to cry tears of frustration and to give up (I've been there!).

But, as I kept telling Beth, when they have those days they haven't forgotten everything they know. They are simply having a bad day.

Just keep moving forward, working at the dog's pace, and recognizing there will be days like that.

Beth's a battler and wasn't going to give up. She continued to do the work and to deal with the bad days when they inevitably happened.

It's all been so worth. They payoff is that Beth can now leave Otis for four hours.

The lockdowns of 2020 and 2021 did caused a wobble for lots of dogs. But Beth knew to just keep Otis flexing that home-alone muscle. He didn't wobble and continues to ace those long absences.

Now let's look at **success stories from my Certified SA Pros.**

- Jessica Ring with Dave and Milo
- Jackie Johnston with Donna and Spark
- Stacey Bell with Jane and Buddy
- Victoria Blondin with Terri and Emma

SA PRO TRAINER
Jessica Ring with Dave and Milo

Milo was already a student in Jessica's online puppy class when Milo's family sought Jessica's help with his home-alone issues

They'd already ditched the crate and had tried to confine with a baby gate or in a bedroom, but he still panicked. He howled, peed, pooped, and vomited.

They noticed his panic at being left very early and immediately started to manage absences.

Jessica started them off on a training plan with a four-minute target duration. She also had them work on Door Is a Bore.

He aced the early absences, so they progressed with increasingly chunky jumps for the target duration. Within a couple of weeks, Milo had reached the 15-minute mark.

The next test was to see how Milo did with the car being driven off. He aced that test too!

By the end of the first month of working with Jessica, Milo had achieved a target duration of 90 minutes. (Do know that that sort of progress is quick, though not unheard of, with puppies.)

Way to go, Team Milo, for knocking it out of the park!

Jessica Ring is the owner of *My Fantastic Friend* (myfantasticfriend.com). Jessica helps you bring out the best in your dog for a happier life together. She offers private and group training for puppies, basic skills, separation anxiety, tricks, and enrichment, as well as consultations for behavior problems.

SA PRO TRAINER
Jackie Johnston with Donna and Spark

Donna adopted adorable rescue mutt (Staffie/boxer/chow) Spark when Spark was approximately three months old. Almost immediately, Donna realized that Spark could not be left alone. Donna immediately put arrangements in place so that Spark would have company at all times.

Donna reached out to Jackie, who got Team Spark started with a gradual exposure training plan. At the same time, she contacted her vet, who prescribed anxiety medication for Spark. When she started out, Spark could only handle three seconds. Within three months of working with Jackie, they progressed to a full four hours! Jackie handed them their wings and let them fly solo.

Donna attributes the success to following Jackie's incremental training program and also to medication, which Donna believes helped Spark learn to be calm during absences.

Spark continues to beat his own records, and Donna is now eyeing a five-hour calm absence. Donna says, "This seems incredible, considering that at the beginning even a five-minute calm absence was impossible." Donna contributes the success to following Jackie's incremental training program and also to medication, which Donna believes helped Spark learn to be calm during absences.

Jackie Johnston is the owner of *Believe in Your Dog* (www.believeinyour.dog) and holds multiple dog training credentials. She works solely with separation anxiety and other alone-time behaviors. Having focused her knowledge and experience in this challenging area, she understands the havoc that this behavior problem can wreak on a dog owner's life and peace of mind.

SA PRO TRAINER
Stacey Bell with Jane and Buddy

Buddy, a cute havanese, and his mom, Jane, started working with SA Pro Stacey when Buddy was six months old and still very much a puppy.

Buddy came from a reputable breeder but had always struggled with alone time.

Stacey started Buddy and Jane on some repetitions of Door Is a Bore. However, Stacey found that Buddy really struggled with the movement, so she added Magic Mat training.

Magic Mat helped Buddy learn that being away from Jane was very rewarding. With Buddy holding his place on the mat, Jane was able to move to and from the door, gradually desensitizing Buddy to door opening.

Adding Magic Mat also helped Buddy settle more easily during departure exercises— especially if there was a sunspot!

Stacey also worked on Buddy's request barking, as this was really straining Jane and Buddy's relationship. Jane was struggling with being able to get through her work Zoom calls.

Stacey guided Jane and Buddy to three minutes of alone time, and they continued the training on their own. These days Buddy aces a cool five or six hours.

Stacey Bell runs *Focused Fun* (www.focusedfun.net) and is obsessed with separation anxiety in dogs! She is dedicated to using a positive, science-based approach to helping dogs overcome separation anxiety.

SA PRO TRAINER
Victoria Blondin with Terri and Emma

When Terri first contacted Victoria, Emma the goldendoodle was 10 months old and Terri had never been able to leave her.

Victoria started Emma and Terri on Door Is a Bore training, but Emma was very stressed even at these steps.

She also started Emma's mom on some short departures (four seconds) and live coached Terri so that Victoria could alert Terri to any stress she saw.

Victoria set up a weekly training schedule for Emma and Terri, which Terri fully adhered to.

In addition to departure training, Victoria recommended that Terri used the Spread the Love protocol. This allowed mom Terri to actually shower in peace (as long as the rest of the family stayed with Emma). Previous to Spread the Love, Emma had to be in the same room as Terri at all times.

Within three weeks of starting work with Victoria, Emma was had spread her love to other family members. Her previous hyper-vigilance stopped, and she was able to settle when mom was out. Emma even began to sleep during absence training.

Emma was able to handle seven minutes of alone time by the time Victoria had finished working with her and Terri. She continues to gain more and more confidence. She can be alone by herself in the kitchen with her mom out front gardening or in the basement for 20 minutes now. The slow, steady progress that Emma has made is exactly the type of improvement that leads to long-term success.

Victoria owns *Shaggy Dog Pet Services* (www.shaggydogpetservice.com) and is a positive force-free trainer. She has a master's degree in animal welfare and behavior as well as a veterinary degree. Victoria helps with many problem behaviors and obedience, but separation anxiety training has always been a huge passion, and she is always ready to help with this tough condition.

INDEX

YOU DON'T HAVE TO DO THIS ALONE!

Now that you've finished the book you're hopefully raring to start the training. If so, you might like to know that you don't have to train on your own. There are a number of ways you can get support with your training.

1. **Join my membership group, Separation Anxiety Heroes,** the unique training club that's just for separation anxiety. You get access to:

- 🐾 the exclusive separation anxiety training app, which will write all your training plans for you,
- 🐾 support from me via my invitation-only Facebook group.

> **LEARN MORE AT**
> **www.subthresholdtraining.com**

2. **Work with one of my SA Pros,** trainers I've personally trained in my method.

3. **Become a member of my free community,** Dog Separation Anxiety Support on Facebook.

4. **Prefer working on your own?** Lots of people do and this book has everything you need.

ABOUT THE AUTHOR

Julie Naismith helps owners and dogs around the world overcome separation anxiety and get their life back on track. While most dog professionals work across a range of cases, Julie is one of the few who focuses on a niche.

Julie's specialist knowledge means that she's come across hundreds of different separation anxiety cases and fully appreciates the nuances of this complex behavioral condition.

Not only does Julie help thousands of dogs and their families, her global SA Pro Certification program trains trainers in her method so that, they too, can help dogs overcome separation anxiety.

Julie acquired her skills and knowledge at the Academy for Dog Trainers, often referred to as the Harvard for dog trainers, where she was taught by world-renowned trainer Jean Donaldson.

Originally from Yorkshire, England, Julie currently lives in the Canadian Rockies with her husband and three dogs.

For more information on Julie's programs for owners or for trainers visit: www.subthresholdtraining.com.

Printed in Great Britain
by Amazon

79546301R00192